interchange
FIFTH EDITION

intro A

Student's Book

Jack C. Richards

WITH DIGITAL PACK

Shaftesbury Road, Cambridge CB2 8EA, United Kingdom

One Liberty Plaza, 20th Floor, New York, NY 10006, USA

477 Williamstown Road, Port Melbourne, VIC 3207, Australia

314–321, 3rd Floor, Plot 3, Splendor Forum, Jasola District Centre, New Delhi – 110025, India

103 Penang Road, #05–06/07, Visioncrest Commercial, Singapore 238467

Cambridge University Press & Assessment is a department of the University of Cambridge.

We share the University's mission to contribute to society through the pursuit of education, learning and research at the highest international levels of excellence.

www.cambridge.org
Information on this title: www.cambridge.org/9781009040563

© Cambridge University Press & Assessment 2013, 2017

This publication is in copyright. Subject to statutory exception and to the provisions of relevant collective licensing agreements, no reproduction of any part may take place without the written permission of Cambridge University Press & Assessment.

First published 2013
Fifth edition 2017
Fifth edition update published 2021

20 19 18 17 16 15 14 13 12 11 10 9 8 7 6 5 4

Printed in Poland by Opolgraf

A catalogue record for this publication is available from the British Library

ISBN 978-1-009-04041-9 Intro Student's Book with eBook
ISBN 978-1-009-04042-6 Intro Student's Book A with eBook
ISBN 978-1-009-04043-3 Intro Student's Book B with eBook
ISBN 978-1-009-04055-6 Intro Student's Book with Digital Pack
ISBN 978-1-009-04056-3 Intro Student's Book A with Digital Pack
ISBN 978-1-009-04057-0 Intro Student's Book B with Digital Pack
ISBN 978-1-316-62237-7 Intro Workbook
ISBN 978-1-316-62239-1 Intro Workbook A
ISBN 978-1-316-62240-7 Intro Workbook B
ISBN 978-1-108-40605-5 Intro Teacher's Edition
ISBN 978-1-316-62221-6 Intro Class Audio
ISBN 978-1-009-04058-7 Intro Full Contact with Digital Pack
ISBN 978-1-009-04059-4 Intro Full Contact A with Digital Pack
ISBN 978-1-009-04062-4 Intro Full Contact B with Digital Pack
ISBN 978-1-108-40304-7 Presentation Plus Intro

Additional resources for this publication at cambridgeone.org

Cambridge University Press & Assessment has no responsibility for the persistence or accuracy of URLs for external or third-party internet websites referred to in this publication, and does not guarantee that any content on such websites is, or will remain, accurate or appropriate. Information regarding prices, travel timetables, and other factual information given in this work is correct at the time of first printing but Cambridge University Press & Assessment does not guarantee the accuracy of such information thereafter.

Informed by teachers

Teachers from all over the world helped develop *Interchange Fifth Edition*. They looked at everything – from the color of the designs to the topics in the conversations – in order to make sure that this course will work in the classroom. We heard from 1,500 teachers in:

- Surveys
- Focus Groups
- In-Depth Reviews

We appreciate the help and input from everyone. In particular, we'd like to give the following people our special thanks:

Jader Franceschi, **Actúa Idiomas,** Bento Gonçalves, Rio Grande do Sul, Brazil

Juliana Dos Santos Voltan Costa, **Actus Idiomas,** São Paulo, Brazil

Ella Osorio, **Angelo State University,** San Angelo, TX, US

Mary Hunter, **Angelo State University,** San Angelo, TX, US

Mario César González, **Angloamericano de Monterrey, SC,** Monterrey, Mexico

Samantha Shipman, **Auburn High School,** Auburn, AL, US

Linda, **Bernick Language School,** Radford, VA, US

Dave Lowrance, **Bethesda University of California,** Yorba Linda, CA, US

Tajbakhsh Hosseini, **Bezmialem Vakif University,** Istanbul, Turkey

Dilek Gercek, **Bil English,** Izmir, Turkey

erkan kolat, **Biruni University, ELT,** Istanbul, Turkey

Nika Gutkowska, **Bluedata International,** New York, NY, US

Daniel Alcocer Gómez, **Cecati 92,** Guadalupe, Nuevo León, Mexico

Samantha Webb, **Central Middle School,** Milton-Freewater, OR, US

Verónica Salgado, **Centro Anglo Americano,** Cuernavaca, Mexico

Ana Rivadeneira Martínez and Georgia P. de Machuca, **Centro de Educación Continua – Universidad Politécnica del Ecuador,** Quito, Ecuador

Anderson Francisco Guimerães Maia, **Centro Cultural Brasil Estados Unidos,** Belém, Brazil

Rosana Mariano, **Centro Paula Souza,** São Paulo, Brazil

Carlos de la Paz Arroyo, Teresa Noemí Parra Alarcón, Gilberto Bastida Gaytan, Manuel Esquivel Román, and Rosa Cepeda Tapia, **Centro Universitario Angloamericano,** Cuernavaca, Morelos, Mexico

Antonio Almeida, **CETEC,** Morelos, Mexico

Cinthia Ferreira, **Cinthia Ferreira Languages Services,** Toronto, ON, Canada

Phil Thomas and Sérgio Sanchez, **CLS Canadian Language School,** São Paulo, Brazil

Celia Concannon, **Cochise College,** Nogales, AZ, US

Maria do Carmo Rocha and CAOP English team, **Colégio Arquidiocesano Ouro Preto – Unidade Cônego Paulo Dilascio,** Ouro Preto, Brazil

Kim Rodriguez, **College of Charleston North,** Charleston, SC, US

Jesús Leza Alvarado, **Coparmex English Institute,** Monterrey, Mexico

John Partain, **Cortazar,** Guanajuato, Mexico

Alexander Palencia Navas, **Cursos de Lenguas, Universidad del Atlántico,** Barranquilla, Colombia

Kenneth Johan Gerardo Steenhuisen Cera, Melfi Osvaldo Guzman Triana, and Carlos Alberto Algarín Jiminez, **Cursos de Lenguas Extranjeras Universidad del Atlantico,** Barranquilla, Colombia

Jane P Kerford, **East Los Angeles College,** Pasadena, CA, US

Daniela, **East Village,** Campinas, São Paulo

Rosalva Camacho Orduño, **Easy English for Groups S.A. de C.V.,** Monterrey, Nuevo León, Mexico

Adonis Gimenez Fusetti, **Easy Way Idiomas,** Ibiúna, Brazil

Eileen Thompson, **Edison Community College,** Piqua, OH, US

Ahminne Handeri O.L Froede, **Englishouse escola de idiomas,** Teófilo Otoni, Brazil

Ana Luz Delgado-Izazola, **Escuela Nacional Preparatoria 5, UNAM,** Mexico City, Mexico

Nancy Alarcón Mendoza, **Facultad de Estudios Superiores Zaragoza, UNAM,** Mexico City, Mexico

Marcilio N. Barros, **Fast English USA,** Campinas, São Paulo, Brazil

Greta Douthat, **FCI Ashland,** Ashland, KY, US

Carlos Lizárraga González, **Grupo Educativo Anglo Americano, S.C.,** Mexico City, Mexico

Hugo Fernando Alcántar Valle, **Instituto Politécnico Nacional, Escuela Superior de Comercio y Administración-Unidad Santotomás, Celex Esca Santo Tomás,** Mexico City, Mexico

Sueli Nascimento, **Instituto Superior de Educação do Rio de Janeiro,** Rio de Janeiro, Brazil

Elsa F Monteverde, **International Academic Services,** Miami, FL, US

Laura Anand, **Irvine Adult School,** Irvine, CA, US

Prof. Marli T. Fernandes (principal) and Prof. Dr. Jefferson J. Fernandes (pedagogue), **Jefferson Idiomass,** São Paulo, Brazil

Herman Bartelen, **Kanda Gaigo Gakuin,** Tokyo, Japan

Cassia Silva, **Key Languages,** Key Biscayne, FL, US

Sister Mary Hope, **Kyoto Notre Dame Joshi Gakuin,** Kyoto, Japan

Nate Freedman, **LAL Language Centres,** Boston, MA, US

Richard Janzen, **Langley Secondary School,** Abbotsford, BC, Canada

Christina Abel Gabardo, **Language House,** Campo Largo, Brazil

Ivonne Castro, **Learn English International,** Cali, Colombia

Julio Cesar Maciel Rodrigues, **Liberty Centro de Línguas,** São Paulo, Brazil

Ann Gibson, **Maynard High School,** Maynard, MA, US

Martin Darling, **Meiji Gakuin Daigaku,** Tokyo, Japan

Dax Thomas, **Meiji Gakuin Daigaku,** Yokohama, Kanagawa, Japan

Derya Budak, **Mevlana University,** Konya, Turkey

B Sullivan, **Miami Valley Career Technical Center International Program,** Dayton, OH, US

Julio Velazquez, **Milo Language Center,** Weston, FL, US

Daiane Siqueira da Silva, Luiz Carlos Buontempo, Marlete Avelina de Oliveira Cunha, Marcos Paulo Segatti, Morgana Eveline de Oliveira, Nadia Lia Gino Alo, and Paul Hyde Budgen, **New Interchange-Escola de Idiomas,** São Paulo, Brazil

Patrícia França Furtado da Costa, Juiz de Fora, Brazil Patricia Servín

Chris Pollard, **North West Regional College SK,** North Battleford, SK, Canada

Olga Amy, **Notre Dame High School,** Red Deer, Canada

Amy Garrett, **Ouachita Baptist University,** Arkadelphia, AR, US

Mervin Curry, **Palm Beach State College,** Boca Raton, FL, US

Julie Barros, **Quality English Studio,** Guarulhos, São Paulo, Brazil

Teodoro González Saldaña and Jesús Monserrrta Mata Franco, **Race Idiomas,** Mexico City, Mexico

Autumn Westphal and Noga La`or, **Rennert International,** New York, NY, US

Antonio Gallo and Javy Palau, **Rigby Idiomas,** Monterrey, Mexico Tatiane Gabriela Sperb do Nascimento, **Right Way,** Igrejinha, Brazil

Mustafa Akgül, **Selahaddin Eyyubi Universitesi,** Diyarbakır, Turkey

James Drury M. Fonseca, **Senac Idiomas Fortaleza,** Fortaleza, Ceara, Brazil

Manoel Fialho S Neto, **Senac – PE,** Recife, Brazil

Jane Imber, **Small World,** Lawrence, KS, US

Tony Torres, **South Texas College,** McAllen, TX, US

Janet Rose, **Tennessee Foreign Language Institute,** College Grove, TN, US

Todd Enslen, **Tohoku University,** Sendai, Miyagi, Japan

Daniel Murray, **Torrance Adult School,** Torrance, CA, US

Juan Manuel Pulido Mendoza, **Universidad del Atlántico,** Barranquilla, Colombia

Juan Carlos Vargas Millán, **Universidad Libre Seccional Cali,** Cali (Valle del Cauca), Colombia

Carmen Cecilia Llanos Ospina, **Universidad Libre Seccional Cali,** Cali, Colombia

Jorge Noriega Zenteno, **Universidad Politécnica del Valle de México,** Estado de México, Mexico

Aimee Natasha Holguin S., **Universidad Politécnica del Valle de México UPVM,** Tultitlàn Estado de México, Mexico

Christian Selene Bernal Barraza, **UPVM Universidad Politécnica del Valle de México,** Ecatepec, Mexico

Lizeth Ramos Acosta, **Universidad Santiago de Cali,** Cali, Colombia

Silvana Dushku, **University of Illinois Champaign,** IL, US

Deirdre McMurtry, **University of Nebraska – Omaha,** Omaha, NE, US

Jason E Mower, **University of Utah,** Salt Lake City, UT, US

Paul Chugg, **Vanguard Taylor Language Institute,** Edmonton, Alberta, Canada

Henry Mulak, **Varsity Tutors,** Los Angeles, CA, US

Shirlei Strucker Calgaro and Hugo Guilherme Karrer, **VIP Centro de Idiomas,** Panambi, Rio Grande do Sul, Brazil

Eleanor Kelly, **Waseda Daigaku Extension Centre,** Tokyo, Japan

Sherry Ashworth, **Wichita State University,** Wichita, KS, US

Laine Bourdene, **William Carey University,** Hattiesburg, MS, US

Serap Aydın, Istanbul, Turkey

Liliana Covino, Guarulhos, Brazil

Yannuarys Jiménez, Barranquilla, Colombia

Juliana Morais Pazzini, Toronto, ON, Canada

Marlon Sanches, Montreal, Canada

Additional content contributed by Kenna Bourke, Inara Couto, Nic Harris, Greg Manin, Ashleigh Martinez, Laura McKenzie, Paul McIntyre, Clara Prado, Lynne Robertson, Mari Vargo, Theo Walker, and Maria Lucia Zaorob.

Classroom Language Teacher instructions

Plan of Intro Book A

Titles/Topics	Speaking	Grammar
UNIT 1 — PAGES 2–7		
What's your name? Alphabet; greetings and leave-takings; names and titles of address; numbers 0–10, phone numbers, and email addresses	Introducing yourself and friends; saying hello and good-bye; asking for names and phone numbers	Possessive adjectives *my*, *your*, *his*, *her*; the verb *be*; affirmative statements and contractions
UNIT 2 — PAGES 8–13		
Where are my keys? Possessions, classroom objects, personal items, and locations in a room	Naming objects; asking for and giving the locations of objects	Articles *a*, *an*, and *the*; *this/these*, *it/they*; plurals; yes/no and *where* questions with *be*; prepositions of place: *in*, *in front of*, *behind*, *on*, *next to*, and *under*
PROGRESS CHECK — PAGES 14–15		
UNIT 3 — PAGES 16–21		
Where are you from? Cities and countries; adjectives of personality and appearance; numbers 11–103 and ages	Talking about cities and countries; asking for and giving information about place of origin, nationality, first language, and age; describing people	The verb *be*: affirmative and negative statements, yes/no questions, short answers, and Wh-questions
UNIT 4 — PAGES 22–27		
Is this coat yours? Clothing; colors; weather and seasons	Asking about and describing clothing and colors; talking about the weather and seasons; finding the owners of objects	Possessives: adjectives *our* and *their*, pronouns, names, and *whose*; present continuous statements and yes/no questions; conjunctions *and*, *but*, and *so*; placement of adjectives before nouns
PROGRESS CHECK — PAGES 28–29		
UNIT 5 — PAGES 30–35		
What time is it? Clock time; times of the day; everyday activities	Asking for and telling time; asking about and describing current activities	Time expressions: *o'clock*, A.M., P.M., *noon*, *midnight*, *in the morning/afternoon/evening*, *at 7:00/night/midnight*; present continuous Wh-questions
UNIT 6 — PAGES 36–41		
I ride my bike to school. Transportation; family relationships; daily routines; days of the week	Asking for and giving information about how people go to work or school; talking about family members; describing daily and weekly routines	Simple present statements with regular and irregular verbs; simple present yes/no and Wh-questions; time expressions: *early*, *late*, *every day*, *on Sundays/weekends/weekdays*
PROGRESS CHECK — PAGES 42–43		
UNIT 7 — PAGES 44–49		
Does it have a view? Houses and apartments; rooms; furniture	Asking about and describing houses and apartments; talking about the furniture in a room	Simple present short answers; *there is*, *there are*; *there's no*, *there isn't a*, *there are no*, *there aren't any*
UNIT 8 — PAGES 50–55		
Where do you work? Jobs and workplaces	Asking for and giving information about work; giving opinions about jobs; describing workday routines	Simple present Wh-questions with *do* and *does*; placement of adjectives after *be* and before nouns
PROGRESS CHECK — PAGES 56–57		
GRAMMAR PLUS — PAGES 132–149		

Pronunciation/Listening	Writing/Reading	Interchange Activity
Linked sounds Listening for the spelling of names, phone numbers, and email addresses	Writing a list of names, phone numbers, and email addresses	"Celebrity classmates": Introducing yourself to new people **PAGE 114**
Plural -s endings Listening for the locations of objects	Writing the locations of objects	"Find the differences": Comparing two pictures of a room **PAGE 115**
Syllable stress Listening for countries, cities, and languages; listening to descriptions of people	Writing questions requesting personal information	"Let's talk!": Finding out more about your classmates **PAGE 118**
The letters s and sh Listening for descriptions of clothing and colors	Writing questions about what people are wearing	"Celebrity fashions": Describing celebrities' clothing **PAGES 116–117**
Rising and falling intonation Listening for times of the day; listening to identify people's actions	Writing times of the day "Message Me!": Reading an online chat between two friends	"What's wrong with this picture?": Describing what's wrong with a picture **PAGE 119**
Third-person singular -s endings Listening for activities and days of the week	Writing about your weekly routine "What's Your Schedule Like?": Reading about someone's daily schedule	"Class survey": Finding out more about classmates' habits and routines **PAGE 120**
Words with th Listening to descriptions of homes; listening to people shop for furniture	Writing about your dream home "Unique Hotels": Reading about two interesting hotels	"Find the differences": Comparing two apartments **PAGE 121**
Reduction of do Listening to people describe their jobs	Writing about jobs "Dream Jobs": Reading about two unusual jobs	"The perfect job": Figuring out what job is right for you **PAGE 122**

Plan of Intro Book A   vii

1 What's your name?

▸ Say hello and make introductions
▸ Say good-bye and exchange contact information

1 CONVERSATION My name is Joshua Brown.

A Listen and practice.

Joshua: Hello. My name is Joshua Brown.
Isabella: Hi. My name is Isabella Martins.
Joshua: It's nice to meet you, Isabella.
Isabella: Nice to meet you, too.
Joshua: I'm sorry. What's your last name again?
Isabella: It's Martins.

First names	Last names
Joshua	Brown
Isabella	Martins

B **PAIR WORK** Introduce yourself to your partner.

2 SNAPSHOT

Listen and practice.

Names and nicknames

Nicholas Hoult

Nicholas (Nick)   Madison (Maddie)   Jennifer (Jen)
Emily (Em)   Joshua (Josh)   Isabella (Izzy)
Michael (Mike)   William (Will)   Elizabeth (Liz)

Jennifer Lawrence

What are some popular names and nicknames in your country?
Do you have a nickname? What is it?

3 GRAMMAR FOCUS

My, your, his, her

What's **your** name?	**My** name's Carlos.	What**'s** = What **is**
What's **his** name?	**His** name's Joshua.	
What's **her** name?	**Her** name's Isabella.	

GRAMMAR PLUS see page 132

A Complete the conversations. Use *my*, *your*, *his*, or *her*.

1. **A:** Hello. What's ____your____ name?
   B: Hi. _____ name is Carlos. What's _____ name?
   A: _____ name is Akina.

2. **A:** What's _____ name?
   B: _____ name is Ethan.
   A: And what's _____ name?
   B: _____ name is Caroline.

B **PAIR WORK** Practice the conversations with a partner.

4 SPEAKING Spelling names

A Listen and practice.

| A | B | C | D | E | F | G | H | I | J | K | L | M | N | O | P | Q | R | S | T | U | V | W | X | Y | Z |
| a | b | c | d | e | f | g | h | i | j | k | l | m | n | o | p | q | r | s | t | u | v | w | x | y | z |

B **CLASS ACTIVITY** Listen and practice. Then practice with your own names. Make a list of your classmates' names.

A: What's your name?
B: My name is Akina Hayashi.
A: Is that A-K-I-N-A?
B: Yes, that's right.
A: How do you spell your last name? H-A-Y-A-S-H-Y?
B: No, it's H-A-Y-A-S-H-I.

My classmates
Akina Hayashi
Ethan Reed

5 LISTENING Your name, please?

How do you spell the names? Listen and check (✓) the correct answers.

1. ☐ Kate
   ☐ Cate
2. ☐ Erick
   ☐ Eric
3. ☐ Sophia
   ☐ Sofia
4. ☐ Zackary
   ☐ Zachary

6 WORD POWER Titles

A Listen and practice.

> **Miss** Kato (single females) **Ms.** Yong (single or married females)
> **Mrs.** Jones (married females) **Mr.** Rodriguez (single or married males)

B Listen and write the titles.

1. _____ Santos   2. _____ Wilson   3. _____ Park   4. _____ Rossi

7 SPEAKING Saying hello

A Listen and practice.

B CLASS ACTIVITY Go around the class. Greet your classmates formally (with titles) and informally (without titles).

8 CONVERSATION Are you Andrea Clark?

A Listen and practice.

Daniel: Excuse me. Are you Andrea Clark?
Sheila: No, I'm not. She's over there.
Daniel: Oh, I'm sorry.

Lena: Matt? This is your book.
Matt: Oh, thank you. You're in my math class, right?
Lena: Yes, I am. I'm Lena Garza.

Jack: Hey, Christy, this is Ben. He's in our history class.
Christy: Hi, Ben.
Ben: Hi, Christy. Nice to meet you.

B **GROUP WORK** Greet a classmate. Then introduce him or her to another classmate.

"Hey, Eduardo, this is . . ."

9 GRAMMAR FOCUS

The verb *be*

I'm Lena Garza.		**Are you** Andrea Clark?	**I'm** = I am	
You're in my class.		Yes, **I am**. (Yes, I'm.)	**You're** = You are	
She's over there. (**Andrea is** over there.)		No, **I'm not**.	**He's** = He is	
He's in our class. (**Ben is** in our class.)			**She's** = She is	
It's Garza. (**My last name is** Garza.)		How **are you**?	**It's** = It is	
		I'm fine, thanks.		

GRAMMAR PLUS see page 132

A Complete the conversation with the correct words in parentheses. Then practice with a partner.

Ben Hello, Christy. How ___are___ (are / is) you?
Christy _____ (I'm / It's) fine, thanks. _____ (I'm / It's) sorry – what's your name again?
Ben _____ (Is / It's) Ben – Ben Durant.
Christy That's right! Ben, this _____ (is / it's) Joshua Brown. _____ (He's / She's) in our history class.
Ben _____ (I'm / It's) nice to meet you.
Joshua Hi, Ben. I think _____ (I'm / you're) in my English class, too.
Ben Oh, right! Yes, I _____ (am / 'm).

What's your name? **5**

B Complete the conversations. Then practice in groups.

Cara Excuse me. ____Are____ you Alex Lane?
James No, _____ not. My name _____ James Harris. Alex _____ over there.
Cara Oh, sorry.

Cara _____ you Alex Lane?
Alex Yes, I _____.
Cara Hi. _____ Cara Ruiz.
Alex Oh, _____ in my history class, right?
Cara Yes, I _____.
Alex _____ nice to meet you, Cara.

C **CLASS ACTIVITY** Write your name on a piece of paper. Put the papers in a bag. Then take a different paper. Find the other student.

A: Excuse me. Are you Min-ji Cho?
B: No, I'm not. She's over there.
A: Hi. Are you Min-ji Cho?
C: Yes, I am.

10 PRONUNCIATION Linked sounds

▶ Listen and practice. Notice the linked sounds.

I'm‿Isabella.   She's‿over there.   You're‿in my class.

11 SPEAKING Personal information

▶ **A** Listen and practice.

0	1	2	3	4	5	6	7	8	9	10
zero (oh)	one	two	three	four	five	six	seven	eight	nine	ten

▶ **B** **PAIR WORK** Practice these phone numbers and email addresses. Then listen and check your answers.

Jessica Adams
402-555-2301 (work phone)
646-486-1004 (cell phone)
jadams1@cup.org (email address)
at — dot

Ryan Walker
212-924-1764 (home phone)
643-555-2285 (cell phone)
ryan-walker_09@cambridge.org (email address)
dash — underscore

"Her name is Jessica Adams. Her work phone number is four-oh-two, five-five-five, two-three-oh-one. Her cell . . ."

Unit 1

12 LISTENING Contact information

A Isabella and Joshua are making a list of classmates' phone numbers and email addresses. Listen and complete the list.

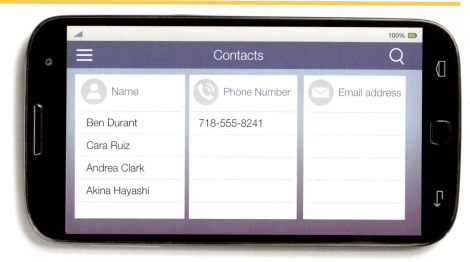

Name	Phone Number	Email address
Ben Durant	718-555-8241	
Cara Ruiz		
Andrea Clark		
Akina Hayashi		

B **CLASS ACTIVITY** Make a list of your classmates' names, phone numbers, and email addresses.

A: What's your name?
B: I'm Maria Ventura.

A: And what's your phone number?
B: It's 323-555-7392.

13 INTERCHANGE 1 Celebrity classmates

Meet some "famous classmates." Go to Interchange 1 on page 114.

14 SPEAKING Saying good-bye

A Listen and practice.

1. Bye, Robin. / See you tomorrow, Preeti.

3. See you later, Mike. / Bye-bye, Mike.

2. Good night, Jake. / Good-bye, Liz. Have a good evening!

4. Good-bye, Mr. Davis. Have a great weekend. / Thank you, Mr. Flores. You, too.

B **CLASS ACTIVITY** Go around the room. Say good-bye to your classmates and teacher.

What's your name? 7

2 Where are my keys?

▸ Identify and discuss personal and classroom objects
▸ Discuss the location of items

1 SNAPSHOT

▶ Listen and practice.

WHAT'S IN YOUR BAG?

☐ a laptop
☐ a cell phone
☐ an umbrella
☐ a wallet
☐ keys
☐ sunglasses
☐ an energy bar
☐ a hairbrush

Check (✓) the things in your bag.
What is one other thing in your bag?

2 ARTICLES Classroom objects

▶ **A** Listen. Complete the sentences with *a* or *an*.

articles
an + vowel sound
a + consonant sound

1. This is _____ book.

4. This is _____ notebook.

2. This is _____ English book.

5. This is _____ pen.

3. This is _____ eraser.

6. This is _____ clock.

B PAIR WORK Find and spell these things in your classroom.

backpack	chair	eraser	pen	notebook
board	desk	pencil	wall	wastebasket
poster	door	outlet	book	window

A: This is a chair.
B: How do you spell *chair*?
A: C-H-A-I-R.

3 CONVERSATION What are these?

▶ Listen and practice.

Brandon: Excuse me. What are these?
Christina: They're flash drives.
Brandon: Oh, they're cool. And what's this?
Christina: It's a tablet.
Brandon: A tablet? Really? Wow! It's great!
Christina: Yes, it is. It's a new model.
Brandon: Huh . . . and what's this?
Christina: It's a tablet case.
Brandon: Oh. It's . . . interesting . . . and different.

4 PRONUNCIATION Plural –s endings

▶ **A** Listen and practice. Notice the pronunciation of the plural –s endings.

s = /z/		s = /s/		(e)s = /ɪz/	
flash drive	flash drive**s**	desk	desk**s**	tablet case	tablet case**s**
cell phone	cell phone**s**	laptop	laptop**s**	class	class**es**
pencil	pencil**s**	backpack	backpack**s**	hairbrush	hairbrush**es**

B Say the plural form of these nouns. Then complete the chart.

 phone case
 student ID
 paper clip
 newspaper
 purse

 tablet
television
 ticket
 box

/z/	/s/	/ɪz/
		phone cases

▶ **C** Listen and check your answers.

5 GRAMMAR FOCUS

▶ *This/these, it/they; plurals*

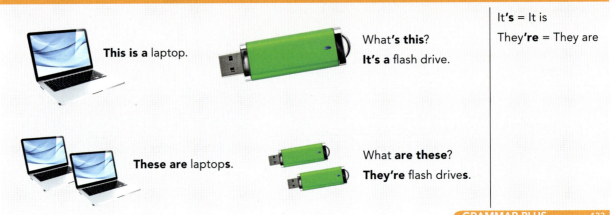

It's = It is
They're = They are

GRAMMAR PLUS see page 133

Complete these conversations. Then practice with a partner.

1. **A:** What ___are these___ ?
   B: _____ .

2. **A:** What _____ ?
   B: _____ .

3. **A:** What _____ ?
   B: _____ .

4. **A:** What _____ ?
   B: _____ .

5. **A:** What _____ ?
   B: _____ .

6. **A:** What _____ ?
   B: _____ .

6 SPEAKING What's this called?

▶ **A** Listen and practice.

A: What's this called in English?
B: I don't know.
C: It's a credit card.
A: How do you spell that?
C: C-R-E-D-I-T C-A-R-D.

A: What are these called in English?
B: I think they're called headphones.
A: How do you spell that?
B: H-E-A-D-P-H-O-N-E-S.

B **GROUP WORK** Choose four things. Put them on a desk.
Then ask about the name and spelling of each thing.

7 CONVERSATION Where are my car keys?

Listen and practice.

Lauren: Oh, no! Where are my car keys?
Matt: I don't know. Are they in your purse?
Lauren: No, they're not.
Matt: Maybe they're on the table in the restaurant.
Server: Excuse me. Are these your keys?
Lauren: Yes, they are. Thank you!
Server: You're welcome. And is this your wallet?
Lauren: Hmm. No, it's not. Where's your wallet, Matthew?
Matt: It's in my pocket. . . . Wait a minute! That *is* my wallet!

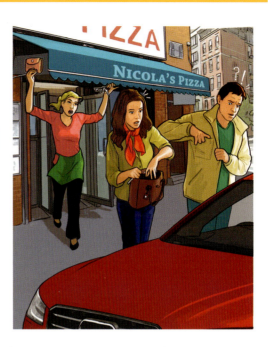

8 GRAMMAR FOCUS

Yes/No and *where* questions with *be*

Is this your wallet?	**Where's** your wallet?
Yes, **it is**. / No, **it's not**.	**It's** in my pocket.
Are these your keys?	**Where are** my keys?
Yes, **they are**. / No, **they're not**.	**They're** on the table.

GRAMMAR PLUS see page 133

A Complete these conversations. Then practice with a partner.

1. **A:** _____Is_____ this your cell phone?
   B: No, _____ not.
   A: _____ these your car keys?
   B: Yes, _____ are. Thanks!

2. **A:** Where _____ my glasses?
   B: Are _____ your glasses?
   A: No, they're _____.
   B: Look! _____ they in your pocket?
   A: Yes, _____. Thanks!

3. **A:** Where _____ your headphones?
   B: _____ on the table.
   A: No, _____ not. They're *my* headphones!
   B: You're right. My headphones _____ in my backpack.

4. **A:** _____ this my umbrella?
   B: No, _____ not. It's my umbrella.
   A: Sorry. _____ is my umbrella?
   B: _____ on your chair.
   A: Oh, you're right!

B GROUP WORK Choose one of your things and put it in a bag. Then choose something from the bag that is not your object. Find the owner of this object.

A: Is this your pen, Akiko?
B: No, it's not.
C: Are these your keys, Marcos?
D: Let me see. Yes, they are.

Where are my keys? 11

9 WORD POWER Prepositions; article *the*

A Listen and practice.

Where is **the** cell phone?
The cell phone is in **the** box.

in

in front of

behind

on

next to

under

B Complete these sentences. Then listen and check your answers.

1. The books are <u>in the backpack</u>.

2. The flash drives are _____.

3. The newspaper is _____.

4. The chair is _____.

5. The wallet is _____.

6. The glasses are _____.

C **PAIR WORK** Ask and answer questions about the pictures in part B.

A: Where are the books?   B: They're in the backpack.

10 LISTENING Emily's things

Listen. Where are Emily's things? Check (✓) the correct locations.

1. sunglasses	☐	on the table	☐	in her purse
2. ID	☐	in her wallet	☐	in front of the clock
3. headphones	☐	on the chair	☐	next to the television
4. tablet	☐	on the table	☐	under the table

Unit 2

11 SPEAKING Where are Kevin's things?

PAIR WORK Help Kevin find his things. Ask and answer questions.

| cell phone | hairbrush | laptop | umbrella | glasses | keys | tablet | credit card |

A: Where's his cell phone?
B: It's under the chair.

12 INTERCHANGE 2 Find the differences

Compare two pictures of a room. Go to Interchange 2 on page 115.

Where are my keys?

Units 1–2 Progress check

SELF-ASSESSMENT

How well can you do these things? Check (✓) the boxes.

I can . . .	Very well	OK	A little
Introduce myself and other people (Ex. 1)	☐	☐	☐
Say hello and good-bye (Ex. 1)	☐	☐	☐
Exchange contact information (Ex. 2)	☐	☐	☐
Understand names for everyday objects and possessions (Ex. 3)	☐	☐	☐
Ask and answer questions about where things are (Ex. 4, 5)	☐	☐	☐

1 SPEAKING How are you?

A Complete the conversation. Use the sentences and questions in the box.

Francisco Hi. How are you?
Nicole I'm fine, thanks. _____
Francisco Pretty good, thanks. _____
Nicole And I'm Nicole White.
Francisco _____
Nicole Nice to meet you, too. _____
Francisco Yes, I am.
Nicole _____
Francisco See you in class.

> My name is Francisco Diaz.
> Oh, are you in my English class?
> How about you?
> ✓ Hi. How are you?
> It's nice to meet you, Nicole.
> Well, have a good day.

B **PAIR WORK** Practice the conversation from part A. Use your own information. Then introduce your partner to a classmate.

"Monica, this is my friend. His name is Kenta. . . ."

2 SPEAKING Is your phone number . . . ?

CLASS ACTIVITY Write your phone number on a piece of paper. Then put the papers in a bag. Take a different paper and find the owner. Write his or her name on the paper.

A: Kamal, is your phone number 781-555-1532?
B: No, it's not. Sorry!
A: Bruna, is your . . . ?

14

3 LISTENING What's this? What are these?

▶ Listen to the conversations. Number the pictures from 1 to 6.

☐ ☐ ☐ ☐ ☐ ☐

4 SPEAKING What's wrong with this room?

A What's wrong with this room? Make a list. Find 10 things.

B PAIR WORK Ask and answer *Where* questions about the picture.

A: Where's the chair?
B: It's on the desk.

5 SPEAKING Yes or No game

Write five yes/no questions about the picture in Exercise 4. Make three questions with "yes" answers and two questions with "no" answers. Then ask a partner the questions.

A: Is the chair behind the clock?
B: No, it isn't.

A: Is the clock in front of the television?
B: Yes, it is.

Units 1–2 Progress check

3 Where are you from?

▶ Discuss cities, countries, nationalities, and languages
▶ Discuss people's appearances, personalities, and ages

1 SNAPSHOT

▶ Listen and practice.

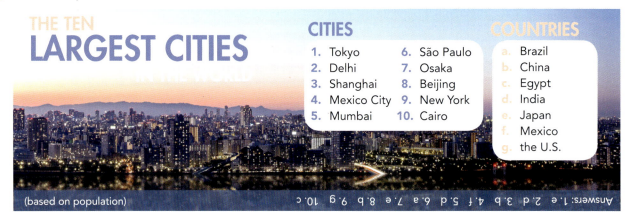

THE TEN LARGEST CITIES

CITIES
1. Tokyo
2. Delhi
3. Shanghai
4. Mexico City
5. Mumbai
6. São Paulo
7. Osaka
8. Beijing
9. New York
10. Cairo

COUNTRIES
a. Brazil
b. China
c. Egypt
d. India
e. Japan
f. Mexico
g. the U.S.

(based on population)

Answers: 1. e 2. d 3. b 4. f 5. d 6. a 7. e 8. b 9. g 10. c

Match the cities with the countries. Then check your answers at the bottom of the Snapshot. What other large cities are in each country? What large cities are in your country?

2 CONVERSATION Are you from Rio?

▶ **A** Listen and practice.

Alexis: Are you from Florida, Felipe?
Felipe: Well, my family is in Florida now, but we're from Brazil originally.
Alexis: Really? My father is Brazilian – from Rio de Janeiro!
Felipe: So, is your first language Portuguese?
Alexis: No, it's English. Are you from Rio?
Felipe: No, we're not. We're from São Paulo.

▶ **B** Listen to Alexis and Felipe talk to Fernando, Nanami, and Sophia. Check (✓) True or False.

	True	False
1. Fernando is from Spain.	☐	☐
2. Nanami is from Japan.	☐	☐
3. Sophia's first language is French.	☐	☐

16

3 GRAMMAR FOCUS

Negative statements and yes/no questions with be

I'm not	from Rio.	Are you	from São Paulo?		I am.		I'm not.
You're not	late.	Am I	early?		you are.		you're not.
She's not	from Japan.	Is she	from the U.S.?		she is.		she's not.
He's not	from Chile.	Is he	from Mexico?	Yes,	he is.	No,	he's not.
It's not	English.	Is it	French?		it is.		it's not.
We're not	from China.	Are you	from South Korea?		we are.		we're not.
You're not	early.	Are we	late?		you are.		you're not.
They're not	in India.	Are they	in Egypt?		they are.		they're not.

We're = we are

GRAMMAR PLUS see page 134

For a list of countries, nationalities, and languages, see the appendix at the back of the book.

A Complete the conversations. Then practice with a partner.

1. **A:** ___Are___ Diana and Mario from Ecuador?
   B: No, _____ not. _____ from Mexico.
   A: _____ you from Mexico, too?
   B: No, _____ not. I'm from Colombia.
   A: So, _____ your first language Spanish?
   B: Yes, it _____.

2. **A:** _____ Meera from England?
   B: No, _____ not. She's from Australia.
   A: _____ she from Sydney?
   B: Yes, she _____. But her parents are from India. _____ not from Australia originally.
   A: _____ Meera's first language Hindi?
   B: No, _____ not. _____ English.

3. **A:** Ji-hye, _____ you and Kwang-ho from South Korea?
   B: Yes, we _____.
   A: And _____ from Seoul?
   B: No, _____ not. _____ from Busan.

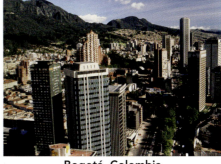
Bogotá, Colombia

Busan, South Korea

B Match the questions with the answers. Then practice with a partner.

1. Are Liam and Grace from England? ___d___
2. Is your first language Mandarin? _____
3. Are you Egyptian? _____
4. Is Mr. Lau from Beijing? _____
5. Is your mother from the U.K.? _____

a. No, he's not. He's from Shanghai.
b. Yes, she is. She's from London.
c. No, it's not. It's Cantonese.
d. No, they're not. They're from New Zealand.
e. Yes, we are. We're from Cairo.

C **PAIR WORK** Write five questions about your classmates. Then ask and answer your questions with a partner.

Where are you from? **17**

4 PRONUNCIATION Syllable stress

A Listen and practice. Notice the syllable stress.

• •	• •	• • •	• • •
China	Brazil	Canada	Malaysia
Turkey	Japan	Mexico	Morocco
_____	_____	_____	_____
_____	_____	_____	_____

B What is the syllable stress in these words? Add the words to the chart in part A. Then listen and check.

English   Spanish   Arabic   Korean
Mexican   Honduras   Chinese   Peru

C **GROUP WORK** Are the words in part A countries, nationalities, or languages? Make a chart and add more words.

Countries	Nationalities	Languages
Brazil	Brazilian	Portuguese
Mexico	Mexican	Spanish

5 SPEAKING Is Bruno Mars from Italy?

A Where are these people from? Check (✓) your guesses.

Bruno Mars
☐ Italy
☐ the Philippines
☐ the U.S.

Morena Baccarin
☐ Argentina
☐ Brazil
☐ the U.S.

Gael García Bernal
☐ Brazil
☐ Mexico
☐ Spain

Mao Asada
☐ China
☐ Japan
☐ South Korea

Chris Hemsworth
☐ Australia
☐ Canada
☐ England

B **PAIR WORK** Compare your guesses. Then check your answers at the bottom of the page.

A: Is Bruno Mars from Italy?
B: No, he's not.
A: Is he from the Philippines?

Answers: 1. the U.S. 2. Brazil 3. Mexico 4. Japan 5. Australia

18 Unit 3

6 CONVERSATION Who's that?

A Listen and practice.

 Nadia Who's that?

 Ben She's my sister.

 Nadia She's really pretty. What's her name?

 Ben Madison. We call her Maddie.

 Nadia Madison . . . that's a beautiful name. How old is she?

 Ben She's twenty-eight.

 Nadia And what's she like? Is she nice?

 Ben Well, she's shy, but she's really kind.

 Nadia And who's that little girl?

 Ben That's her daughter Mia. She's six years old.

 Nadia She's cute!

 Ben Yes, she is – and she's very smart, too.

7 SPEAKING Numbers and ages

A Listen and practice.

11 eleven	**21** twenty-one	**40** forty
12 twelve	**22** twenty-two	**50** fifty
13 thirteen	**23** twenty-three	**60** sixty
14 fourteen	**24** twenty-four	**70** seventy
15 fifteen	**25** twenty-five	**80** eighty
16 sixteen	**26** twenty-six	**90** ninety
17 seventeen	**27** twenty-seven	**100** one hundred
18 eighteen	**28** twenty-eight	**101** one hundred (and) one
19 nineteen	**29** twenty-nine	**102** one hundred (and) two
20 twenty	**30** thirty	**103** one hundred (and) three

B Listen and practice. Notice the word stress.

thirteen – thirty   fourteen – forty   fifteen – fifty   sixteen – sixty

C PAIR WORK Look at the people in Ben's family for one minute. How old are they? Close your books and tell your partner.

A. Carol – 76   **B.** Richard – 50   **C.** Karen – 49   **D.** Amber – 17   **E.** Jay and Joe – 10

Where are you from?   19

8 GRAMMAR FOCUS

▶ Wh-questions with *be*

What's your name?
  My name is Sophia.
Where are you from?
  I'm from Canada.
How are you today?
  I'm fine, thanks.

Who's that?
  She's my sister.
How old is she?
  She's twenty-eight.
What's she like?
  She's very nice.

Who are they?
  They're my classmates.
Where are they from?
  They're from San Francisco.
What's San Francisco like?
  It's very beautiful.

Who**'s** = Who **is**

GRAMMAR PLUS *see page 134*

A Complete the conversations with Wh-questions. Then practice with a partner.

1. **A:** Look! *Who's that* ?
   B: Oh, she's a new student.
   A: _____ ?
   B: I think her name is Yoo-jin.
   A: Yoo-jin? _____ ?
   B: She's from South Korea.

2. **A:** Hi, Brittany. _____ ?
   B: I'm fine, thanks. My friend Leandro is here this week – from Argentina.
   A: Oh, cool. _____ ?
   B: He's really friendly.
   A: _____ ?
   B: He's twenty-five years old.

3. **A:** Azra, _____ ?
   B: I'm from Turkey. From Ankara.
   A: _____ ?
   B: Well, Ankara is the capital of Turkey. It's very old.
   A: _____ ?
   B: My last name is Ganim.

4. **A:** Good morning, Luke. _____ ?
   B: I'm great, thanks.
   A: Cool. _____ ?
   B: They're my friends from school.
   A: _____ ?
   B: They're from Miami, like me.

B **PAIR WORK** Write six Wh-questions about your partner and six Wh-questions about your partner's best friend. Then ask and answer the questions.

Your partner	Your partner's best friend
Where are you from?	Who's your best friend?

20 Unit 3

9 WORD POWER Describing people

A Listen and practice.

a. pretty	d. talkative	g. funny	j. shy	m. heavy
b. handsome	e. friendly	h. quiet	k. short	n. thin
c. good-looking	f. kind	i. serious	l. tall	

B **PAIR WORK** Complete the chart with words from part A. Add two more words to each list. Then describe your personality and appearance to a partner.

Personality	Appearance
talkative ___ ___	pretty ___ ___
___ ___ ___	___ ___ ___
___ ___ ___	___ ___ ___

"I'm tall, friendly, and very talkative."

10 LISTENING Wow! Who's that?

Listen to three descriptions. Check (✓) the two correct words for each description.

1. Nora is . . .	2. Taylor is . . .	3. Austin is . . .
☐ tall	☐ funny	☐ short
☐ pretty	☐ pretty	☐ serious
☐ quiet	☐ handsome	☐ talkative
☐ talkative	☐ serious	☐ tall

11 INTERCHANGE 3 Let's talk!

Talk to your classmates. Go to Interchange 3 on page 118.

Where are you from?

4 Is this coat yours?

▸ **Discuss work and free-time clothes; colors**
▸ **Discuss the weather and what people are wearing**

1 WORD POWER Clothes

▸ **A** Listen and practice.

Clothes for work

jacket
shirt
blouse
tie
suit
belt
pants
skirt
raincoat
dress
shoes
coat
high heels

Clothes for free time

hat
T-shirt
scarf
gloves
sweater
shorts
jeans
boots
socks
sneakers
pajamas
cap
swimsuits

B Complete the chart with words from part A.

Clothes for warm weather	Clothes for cold weather
86°F | 30°C	32°F | 0°C

C **PAIR WORK** Look around the classroom. What clothes do you see? Tell a partner.

"I see jeans, a sweater, boots, and . . ."

22

2 SPEAKING Colors

A Listen and practice.

white	light gray	gray
dark gray	beige	light brown
brown	dark brown	black

B GROUP WORK Ask about favorite colors.

A: What are your favorite colors?
B: My favorite colors are orange and dark blue.

C GROUP WORK Describe the clothes in Exercise 1.

A: The suit is black.
B: The socks are dark blue.

3 PRONUNCIATION The letters s and sh

A Listen and practice. Notice the pronunciation of **s** and **sh**.

suit   **s**ocks   **s**wimsuit
shirt   **sh**orts   **sh**oes

B Read the sentences. Pay attention to the pronunciation of **s** and **sh**.

1. This is Jo**sh**ua's new **s**uit.
2. These are **S**arah's purple **sh**oes!
3. Where are my **sh**oes and **s**ocks?
4. My **sh**orts and T-**sh**irts are blue!

4 CONVERSATION Whose jeans are these?

Listen and practice.

Ashley: Great! Our clothes are dry.
Jessica: Hey, where is my new blouse?
Ashley: What color is your blouse? Is this yours?
Jessica: No, this blouse is blue. Mine is white. Wait! It *is* mine. My white blouse is . . . blue!
Ashley: Oh, no! Look. It's a disaster! *All* our clothes are blue . . .
Jessica: Here's the problem. It's these blue jeans. Whose jeans are these? Are they yours?
Ashley: Uh, yes, they're mine. Sorry.

Is this coat yours? 23

5 GRAMMAR FOCUS

Possessives

Adjectives	Pronouns	Names	
my	mine.	Jack's tie.	s = /s/
your	yours.	Taylor's shoes.	s = /z/
These are **his** shoes.	These shoes are **his**.	Alex's coat.	s = /ɪz/
her	hers.		
our	ours.	Whose tie is this? It's **Greg's**.	
their	theirs.	Whose shoes are these? They're **Taylor's**.	

GRAMMAR PLUS see page 135

A Complete the conversations with the correct words in parentheses. Then practice with a partner.

1. **A:** This isn't ___my___ (my / mine) raincoat. Is it _____ (your / yours)?
   B: No, it's not _____ (my / mine). Ask Emma. Maybe it's _____ (her / hers).

2. **A:** Hey! These aren't _____ (our / ours) sneakers!
   B: You're right. _____ (Our / Ours) are over there.

3. **A:** Are these _____ (your / yours) gloves, Erin?
   B: No, they're not _____ (my / mine). Maybe they are Logan's. _____ (His / Your) gloves are gray.

4. **A:** _____ (Whose / Yours) T-shirts are these? Are they Hayley's and Brad's?
   B: No, they're not _____ (their / theirs) T-shirts. _____ (Their / Theirs) are white, not blue.

B **CLASS ACTIVITY** Put one of your things in a box. Then choose a different thing from the box. Go around the class and find the owner.

A: Laura, are these sunglasses yours?
B: No, they're not mine. Maybe they're Joon-ho's.
C: Wei, is this your pen?
D: Yes, it is.

6 LISTENING Her sneakers are purple.

A Listen to someone describe six people. Number the pictures from 1 to 6 in the order you hear them.

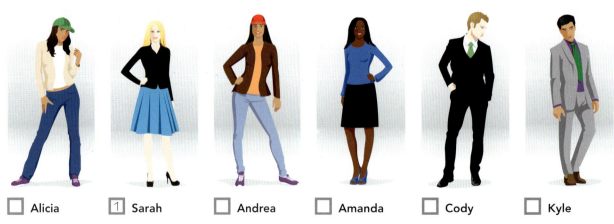

☐ Alicia   ☐ 1 Sarah   ☐ Andrea   ☐ Amanda   ☐ Cody   ☐ Kyle

B **PAIR WORK** Now talk about the people. What colors are their clothes?

A: What color is Alicia's jacket?
B: It's beige.

7 SNAPSHOT

▶ Listen and practice.

WEATHER AND SEASONS AROUND THE WORLD

It's spring in São Paulo, Brazil. It's warm. It's very sunny.

It's summer in Seoul, South Korea. It's raining. It's hot and humid.

It's fall in Chicago in the U.S. It's cool. It's cloudy and windy.

It's winter in Toronto, Canada. It's snowing. It's very cold.

What season is it now in your town or city? What's the weather like today?
What's your favorite season?

8 CONVERSATION Are you wearing your gloves?

▶ Listen and practice.

Ashley Oh, no!
Jessica What's the matter?
Ashley It's snowing! Wow, it's so cold and windy!
Jessica Are you wearing your gloves?
Ashley No, I'm not. They're at home.
Jessica What about your scarf?
Ashley It's at home, too.
Jessica Well, you're wearing your coat.
Ashley But my coat isn't very warm. And I'm not wearing boots!
Jessica OK. Let's take a taxi.
Ashley Good idea!

Is this coat yours? **25**

9 GRAMMAR FOCUS

Present continuous statements; conjunctions

		OR:	
I**'m**	I**'m not**		
You**'re**	You**'re not**	You **aren't**	
She**'s wearing shoes.**	She**'s not**	She **isn't wearing boots.**	
We**'re**	We**'re not**	We **aren't**	
They**'re**	They**'re not**	They **aren't**	
It**'s snowing.**	It**'s not**	It **isn't raining.**	

Conjunctions

It's snowing, **and** it's windy.
It's sunny, **but** it's cold.
It's windy, **so** it's very cold.

GRAMMAR PLUS see page 135

A Complete these sentences from a travel show on TV. Then compare with a partner.

My name is Dylan Jones. I <u>'m wearing</u> a new gray suit. I _____ new black shoes, too. It's raining, but I _____ a raincoat.

It's very hot and sunny today. Michael _____ light blue shorts and white sneakers. He _____ a white T-shirt, but he _____ a cap.

Adriana Fuentes is from Mexico. She _____ a pretty yellow dress and a brown belt. She _____ high heels and a light brown jacket, but she _____ a coat. Wow, it's really windy!

Hee-sun and Kun-woo are here with me today. They're 10 years old. It's really cold, so they _____ winter clothes. They _____ boots, gloves, hats, and scarves. And they _____ heavy coats!

26 Unit 4

> **Present continuous yes/no questions**

Are you **wearing** gloves?	Yes, I **am**.	No, I**'m not**.
Is she **wearing** boots?	Yes, she **is**.	No, she**'s not**./No, she **isn't**.
Are they **wearing** sunglasses?	Yes, they **are**.	No, they**'re not**./No, they **aren't**.

GRAMMAR PLUS *see page 135*

B PAIR WORK Ask and answer these questions about the people in part A.

1. Is Dylan wearing a gray suit?
2. Is he wearing a raincoat?
3. Is he wearing black shoes?
4. Is Michael wearing jeans?
5. Is he wearing a T-shirt?
6. Is he wearing a cap?
7. Is Adriana wearing a skirt?
8. Is she wearing a jacket?
9. Is she wearing high heels?
10. Are Hee-sun and Kun-woo wearing swimsuits?
11. Are they wearing gloves and hats?
12. Are they wearing sneakers?

A: Is Dylan wearing a gray suit?
B: Yes, he is. Is he wearing a raincoat?
A: No, he's not. OR No, he isn't.

> **adjective + noun**
>
> My suit is **black**.
> I'm wearing **a black suit**.

C Write four more questions about the people in part A. Then ask a partner the questions.

10 LISTENING You look great in pink.

A Listen. What are their names? Write the names **Brittany**, **Ryan**, **John**, **Robert**, **Kayla**, and **Amber** in the correct boxes.

B GROUP WORK Ask questions about the people in the picture.

A: Is John wearing a brown jacket?
B: Yes, he is.
C: Is he wearing a cap?

C GROUP WORK Write five questions about your classmates. Then ask and answer the questions.

> Are Maria and Bruno wearing jeans?
> Is Bruno wearing a red shirt?

11 INTERCHANGE 4 Celebrity fashions

What are your favorite celebrities wearing? Go to Interchange 4 on pages 116–117.

Is this coat yours? 27

Units 3–4 Progress check

SELF-ASSESSMENT

How well can you do these things? Check (✓) the boxes.

I can . . .	Very well	OK	A little
Ask and answer questions about countries of origin, nationalities, and languages (Ex. 1)	☐	☐	☐
Understand descriptions of people (Ex. 2)	☐	☐	☐
Ask and answer questions about people's appearance and personality (Ex. 2, 5)	☐	☐	☐
Ask and answer questions about people's possessions (Ex. 3)	☐	☐	☐
Talk and write about my and other people's favorite things (Ex. 4)	☐	☐	☐
Ask and answer questions about what people are wearing (Ex. 5)	☐	☐	☐

1 SPEAKING Interview with my classmates

Match the questions with the answers. Then ask and answer the questions with a partner. Answer with your own information.

1. Are you from Argentina? __h__
2. Where are you and your family from? _____
3. What is your hometown like? _____
4. Is English your first language? _____
5. Who is your best friend? _____
6. How old is your best friend? _____
7. Is our teacher from the U.S.? _____
8. Are our classmates friendly? _____

a. It's very beautiful.
b. Yes, she is.
c. We're from Montevideo.
d. My best friend is Takuya.
e. Yes, they are.
f. No, it's not. It's Spanish.
g. He's nineteen.
h. No, I'm not. I'm from Uruguay.

2 LISTENING Where's your friend Jacob?

A Listen to four conversations. Check (✓) the correct description for each person. You will check more than one adjective.

1. Jacob
☐ tall
☐ short
☐ funny
☐ serious
☐ nice
☐ shy

2. Monica
☐ tall
☐ talkative
☐ pretty
☐ shy
☐ nice
☐ friendly

3. Hannah
☐ thin
☐ short
☐ quiet
☐ shy
☐ serious
☐ funny

4. Ki-nam
☐ tall
☐ short
☐ funny
☐ friendly
☐ talkative
☐ quiet

B Write five yes/no questions about the people in part A. Then ask a partner the questions.

Is Jacob tall?
Is Monica thin?

3 SPEAKING Are these your clothes?

CLASS ACTIVITY Draw three pictures of clothes on different pieces of paper. Then put the papers in a bag. Take three different papers, go around the class, and find the owners.

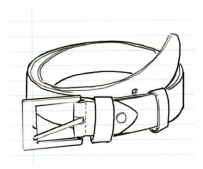

A: Anna, is this your belt?
B: No, it's not mine. Maybe it's Miki's.

A: Ji-hun, are these your sneakers?
C: Yes, they're mine. Thanks!

4 SPEAKING Similar or different?

A Write your favorite things in the chart. Then ask a partner about his or her favorite things. Write them in the chart.

Favorite	Me	My partner
1. season		
2. color		
3. clothes		

B Compare answers. What's the same? What's different? Write sentences.

> Spring is my favorite season, and it's Mariana's favorite season. That's the same.
> My favorite color is green, but Mariana's favorite color is red, so that's different.

5 SPEAKING I'm thinking of . . .

GROUP WORK Think of a student in the class. Your classmates ask yes/no questions to guess the student.

A: I'm thinking of a student in this class.
B: Is it a woman?
A: Yes, it is.
C: Is she short?
A: No, she isn't.
D: Is she wearing blue jeans?

WHAT'S NEXT?

Look at your Self-assessment again. Do you need to review anything?

Units 3–4 Progress check

5 What time is it?

▸ Discuss cities and time zones
▸ Discuss people's activities

1 SNAPSHOT

▶ Listen and practice.

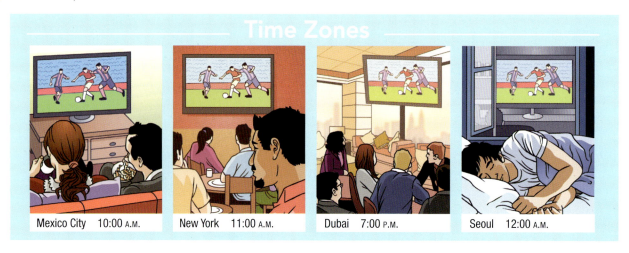

Time Zones

Mexico City 10:00 A.M.   New York 11:00 A.M.   Dubai 7:00 P.M.   Seoul 12:00 A.M.

Is your city or town in the same time zone as one of these cities?
What other events or shows are on television in different time zones?

2 CONVERSATION It's two o'clock in the morning!

▶ **A** Listen and practice.

2:00 A.M. ▾

Amar: Hello?
Brian: Hi, Amar! This is Brian. I'm calling from New York.
Amar: Brian? Wait. . . . Where are you?
Brian: I'm home on vacation, remember? I'm calling about the soccer game. Great game!
Amar: Oh, that's good. But what time is it there?
Brian: It's 2:00 P.M. And it's two o'clock in Australia, too. Right?
Amar: That's right – it's two o'clock in the morning!
Brian: 2:00 A.M.? Oh, of course! I'm really sorry.
Amar: That's OK. Congratulations on the game!

2:00 P.M. ▴

30

3 GRAMMAR FOCUS

▶ What time is it?

 It's two **o'clock**.

 It's two-oh-five.
It's five **after** two.

 It's two-fifteen.
It's **a quarter after** two.

 It's two-thirty.

 It's two-forty.
It's twenty **to** three.

 It's two forty-five.
It's **a quarter to** three.

GRAMMAR PLUS *see page 136*

A PAIR WORK Look at these clocks. What time is it?

1   2   3   4   5   6

A: What time is it?
B: It's ten after ten. OR It's ten-ten.

▶ Is it A.M. or P.M.?

It's six (o'clock) **in the morning**.
It's 6:00 A.M.

It's twelve (o'clock).
It's 12:00 P.M.
It's **noon**.

It's four (o'clock) **in the afternoon**.
It's 4:00 P.M.

It's six (o'clock) **in the evening**.
It's 6:00 P.M.

It's nine (o'clock) **at night**.
It's 9:00 P.M.

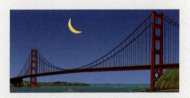
It's twelve (o'clock) **at night**.
It's 12:00 A.M.
It's **midnight**.

GRAMMAR PLUS *see page 136*

B PAIR WORK Say each time a different way.

1. It's eight o'clock in the morning. *"It's 8:00 A.M."*
2. It's three o'clock in the afternoon.
3. It's six o'clock in the evening.
4. It's twelve o'clock at night.
5. It's 10:00 A.M.
6. It's 4:00 P.M.
7. It's 7:00 P.M.
8. It's 12:00 P.M.

What time is it? **31**

4 LISTENING What time is it in Tokyo?

A Lauren and John are calling friends in different parts of the world. Listen. What time is it in these cities?

City	Time
Vancouver	4:00 P.M.
Bangkok	
London	
Tokyo	
São Paulo	

B Listen again. Check (✓) the correct answers.

1. Tanawat is . . . ☐ getting married. ☐ in São Paulo. ☐ sleeping.
2. Richard is . . . ☐ in London. ☐ in Bangkok. ☐ late.
3. Misaki is . . . ☐ in Tokyo. ☐ in Vancouver. ☐ watching TV.

5 CONVERSATION What are you doing?

Listen and practice.

JAY Hey, Kate!

KATE What are you doing?

JAY I'm cooking.

KATE I know, but why are you cooking now? It's three o'clock in the morning!

JAY I'm sorry, but I'm really hungry.

KATE Hmm . . . What are you making?

JAY Spaghetti.

KATE With tomato sauce?

JAY With tomato sauce and cheese.

KATE I love spaghetti! Uh . . . I'm getting hungry, too.

JAY Good. Let's eat!

6 PRONUNCIATION Rising and falling intonation

A Listen and practice. Notice the intonation of the yes/no and Wh-questions.

Is he cooking?   What's he making?
Are they sleeping?   What are they doing?

B Listen to the questions. Draw a rising arrow (↗) for rising intonation and a falling arrow (↘) for falling intonation.

1. ↗   2. _____   3. _____   4. _____   5. _____   6. _____

32 Unit 5

7 GRAMMAR FOCUS

Present continuous Wh-questions

San Diego   4:00 A.M.

What's Daniel **doing**?
He**'s sleeping** right now.

Guadalajara   6:00 A.M.

What's Leticia **doing**?
It's 6:00 A.M., so she**'s getting up**.

Washington, D.C.   7:00 A.M.

What are Lya and Erin **doing**?
They're having breakfast.

Brasilia   9:00 A.M.

What's Tiago **doing**?
He**'s going** to work.

Edinburgh   noon

What are Kim and Paul **doing**?
It's noon, so they**'re eating** lunch.

Cairo   3:00 P.M.

What's Amina **doing**?
She**'s working**.

Jakarta   7:00 P.M.

What's Tamara **doing**?
She**'s eating** dinner right now.

Osaka   9:00 P.M.

What's Kento **doing**?
He**'s checking** his messages.

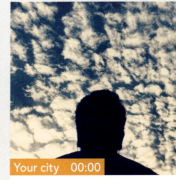

Your city   00:00

What are you **doing**?
It's . . . I**'m** . . .

GRAMMAR PLUS see page 136

A PAIR WORK Ask and answer the questions about the pictures.

1. Who's having breakfast?
2. Who's eating dinner?
3. Where's Amina working?
4. Where's Kento checking his messages?
5. What's Daniel doing?
6. What's Tiago wearing?
7. Why is Leticia getting up?
8. Why are Kim and Paul having lunch?

spelling

sleep → sleep**ing**
get → get**ting** (+ t)
have → hav**ing** (– e)

B GROUP WORK Write five more questions about the pictures. Then ask and answer your questions in groups.

What time is it?   33

8 WORD POWER What are they doing?

A Listen and practice. *"They're dancing."*

dance   drive   listen to music   play basketball

read   ride a bike   run   shop

study   swim   take a walk   watch a movie

B **PAIR WORK** Ask and answer questions about the pictures in part A.

A: Are they running?
B: No, they're not.

A: What are they doing?
B: They're dancing.

C **GROUP WORK** Make two teams. Write an activity on a piece of paper. Give the paper to the other team. Two members act out each activity. Their team guesses. Can they guess the activity?

A: Are you running?
B: No, we're not.

C: Are you riding bikes?
D: Yes, we are!

riding bikes

9 INTERCHANGE 5 What's wrong with this picture?

What's wrong with this picture? Go to Interchange 5 on page 119.

34 Unit 5

10 READING

A Skim the conversation. Write the name of the correct person on each picture.

MESSAGE ME!

Eva and Pam are friends. They message on social media every day. Pam lives in Atlanta, in the United States. Eva is visiting friends in Puebla, Mexico.

Profile   Photos   Share   Find Friends

Eva35 Hey! How are you today, Pam?

PamL Hi, Eva! I'm fine, thanks. What are you doing?

Eva35 I'm sitting on the couch watching a movie. It's great!

PamL Lucky you! I'm writing a report. It's for my job.

Eva35 Oh, really? Are you at your office?

PamL Yeah. My friend Lety is making me coffee. She's helping me with the report.

Eva35 Cool. I'm . . . Oh, wait. My cell phone is ringing. Be right back. Sorry. It's my friend, Paul. He's making lunch.

PamL Right. I have to go, Eva. Sorry. My boss is calling me.

Eva35 OK. Good luck with the report! Have a good evening!

PamL Thanks, Eva. Enjoy your movie!

B Read the conversation. Who is doing these things? Choose the correct answers.

1. Pam   Eva   . . . is watching a movie.
2. Eva   Pam   . . . is visiting friends.
3. Pam   Eva   . . . is working in an office.
4. Lety   Paul   . . . is making coffee.
5. Paul   Pam   . . . is calling Eva on her cell phone.
6. Eva   Pam's boss . . . is calling Pam.

C PAIR WORK Think about online conversations you have with friends. What do you say? What do you ask about? Write a short conversation.

What time is it? 35

6 I ride my bike to school.

▸ Discuss transportation and family
▸ Discuss daily and weekly routines

1 SNAPSHOT

▶ Listen and practice.

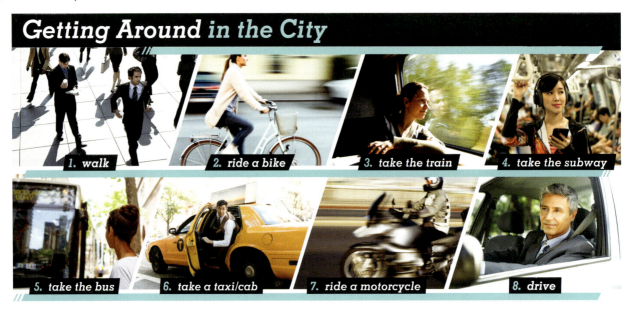

Getting Around in the City

1. walk
2. ride a bike
3. take the train
4. take the subway
5. take the bus
6. take a taxi/cab
7. ride a motorcycle
8. drive

Check (✓) the kinds of transportation you use.
What are some other kinds of transportation?

2 CONVERSATION They use public transportation.

▶ Listen and practice.

Yuto: Nice car, Austin! Is it yours?
Austin: No, it's my sister's. She has a new job and she drives to work.
Yuto: Is her job here in the suburbs?
Austin: No, it's downtown.
Yuto: My parents work downtown, but they don't drive to work. They use public transportation.
Austin: The bus or the train?
Yuto: The bus doesn't stop near our house, so they take the train.

3 WORD POWER Family members

A PAIR WORK Complete the sentences about the Mitchell family. Then listen and check your answers.

1. Lisa is Tom's _____wife_____.
2. Megan and Austin are their _____.
3. Tom is Lisa's _____.
4. Austin is Lisa's _____.
5. Megan is Tom's _____.
6. Austin is Megan's _____.
7. Megan is Austin's _____.
8. Tom and Lisa are Austin's _____.

> kids = children
> mom = mother
> dad = father

B PAIR WORK Who are the people in your family? What are their names?

"My father's name is Arthur. My sisters' names are Emilia and Sabrina."

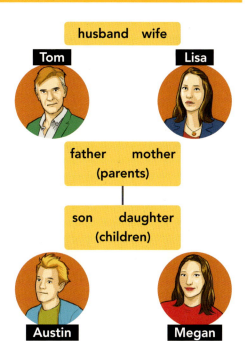

4 GRAMMAR FOCUS

Simple present statements

I	**walk**	to school.	I	**don't live**	far from here.	**don't**	= do not
You	**ride**	your bike to school.	You	**don't live**	near here.	**doesn't**	= does not
He	**works**	near here.	He	**doesn't work**	downtown.		
She	**takes**	the bus to work.	She	**doesn't drive**	to work.		
We	**live**	with our parents.	We	**don't live**	alone.		
They	**use**	public transportation.	They	**don't need**	a car.		

GRAMMAR PLUS see page 137

A Tom Mitchell is talking about his family. Complete the sentences with the correct verb forms. Then compare with a partner.

1. My family and I _____live_____ (live / lives) in the suburbs. My wife and I _____ (work / works) near here, so we _____ (walk / walks) to work. Our daughter Megan _____ (work / works) downtown, so she _____ (drive / drives) to work. Our son _____ (don't / doesn't) drive. He _____ (ride / rides) his bike to school.

2. My parents _____ (live / lives) in the city. My mother _____ (take / takes) the subway to work. My father is retired, so he _____ (don't / doesn't) work now. He also _____ (use / uses) public transportation, so they _____ (don't / doesn't) need a car.

> **verb endings: he, she, it**
>
> walk → walk**s**
> ride → ride**s**
> study → stud**ies**
> watch → watch**es**

I ride my bike to school. **37**

▶ **Simple present statements with irregular verbs**

I/you/we/they
I **have** a bike.
We **do** our homework every day.
My parents **go** to work by train.

he/she/it
My mother **has** a car.
My father **does** a lot of work at home.
The train **goes** downtown.

GRAMMAR PLUS see page 137

B Yuto is talking about his family and his friend Austin. Complete the sentences. Then compare with a partner.

1. My parents _____have_____ (have / has) a house in the suburbs. My mom and dad _____ (go / goes) downtown to work. My parents are very busy, so I _____ (do / does) a lot of work at home.

2. My brother doesn't live with us. He _____ (have / has) an apartment in the city. He _____ (go / goes) to school all day, and he _____ (do / does) his homework at night.

3. I _____ (have / has) a new friend. His name is Austin. We _____ (go / goes) to the same school, and sometimes we _____ (do / does) our homework together.

C **PAIR WORK** Tell your partner about your family.

"I have one brother and two sisters. My brother is a teacher. He has a car, so he drives to work."

5 PRONUNCIATION Third-person singular –s endings

▶ Listen and practice. Notice the pronunciation of the **–s** endings.

s = /s/	**s** = /z/	**(e)s** = /ɪz/	*irregular*
take tak**es**	drive driv**es**	dance danc**es**	do do**es**
sleep sleep**s**	study stud**ies**	watch watch**es**	have ha**s**

6 CONVERSATION What time do you get up?

▶ Listen and practice.

Paige: Let's go to the park Sunday morning.
Adam: Good idea, but let's go in the afternoon. I sleep late on weekends.
Paige: What time do you get up?
Adam: I get up at noon.
Paige: Really? That's late. Do you eat breakfast at noon?
Adam: Yeah. What time do *you* get up?
Paige: At ten o'clock.
Adam: Oh, that's early for a Sunday.
Paige: Hey, I have an idea! Let's eat at Park Café. They serve breakfast all day!

38 Unit 6

7 GRAMMAR FOCUS

Simple present questions

Do you **get up** early on Sundays?
No, I **get up** late.
Does he **eat** breakfast at seven o'clock?
No, he **eats** breakfast at seven-thirty.
Do they **take** a taxi to class?
No, they **take** the bus.

What time do you **get up**?
At noon.
What time does she have dinner?
At eight o'clock.
When do they **take** the subway?
On Mondays and Wednesdays.

GRAMMAR PLUS see page 137

A Complete the questions with *do* or *does*.

1. ___Do___ you get up late on Sundays?
2. _____ you have lunch at home every day?
3. What time _____ your father leave work on Fridays?
4. _____ your mother cook on weekdays?
5. _____ your father shop on Saturdays?
6. _____ you take a walk in the evening?
7. When _____ you listen to music?
8. What time _____ you check your email?
9. What time _____ your parents have dinner?
10. When _____ you study English?
11. _____ your best friend ride a bike on weekends?
12. _____ your father drive to work every morning?

time expressions	
early	**in** the morning
late	**in** the afternoon
every day	**in** the evening
at 9:00	**on** Sundays
at noon/midnight	**on** weekdays
at night	**on** weekends

B PAIR WORK Ask and answer the questions from part A. Use time expressions from the box.

A: Do you get up late on Sundays?
B: No, I don't. I get up at eight o'clock. I play basketball on Sunday mornings.

C Unscramble the questions to complete the conversations. Then ask a partner the questions. Answer with your own information.

1. **A:** _What time do you eat dinner_ ?
   you / what time / dinner / do / eat
   B: At 7:00 P.M.
2. **A:** _____?
   you / every morning / check your messages / do
   B: Yes, I check my messages on the bus every morning.
3. **A:** _____?
   at / start / does / seven o'clock / this class
   B: No, this class starts at eight o'clock.
4. **A:** _____?
   listen to music / you / do / when
   B: I listen to music in the evening.
5. **A:** _____?
   on weekends / you and your friends / do / play sports
   B: Yes, we play volleyball on Saturdays.

I ride my bike to school. **39**

8 LISTENING Kayla's weekly routine

▶ Listen to Kayla talk about her weekly routine. Check (✓) the days she does each thing.

	Monday	Tuesday	Wednesday	Thursday	Friday	Saturday	Sunday
get up early	☐	☐	☐	☐	☐	☐	☐
go to work	☐	☐	☐	☐	☐	☐	☐
play tennis	☐	☐	☐	☐	☐	☐	☐
go shopping	☐	☐	☐	☐	☐	☐	☐
see friends	☐	☐	☐	☐	☐	☐	☐
dinner with family	☐	☐	☐	☐	☐	☐	☐
study	☐	☐	☐	☐	☐	☐	☐

9 SPEAKING My weekly routine

A What do you do every week? Write your routine in the chart.

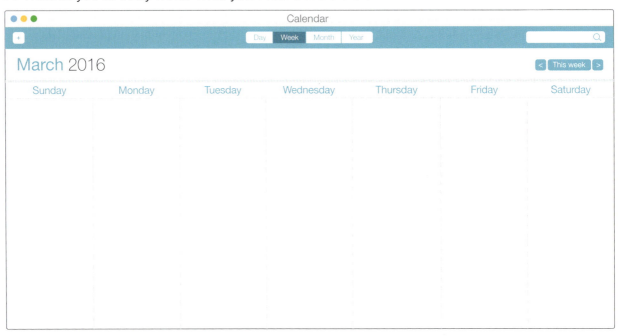

B GROUP WORK Discuss your weekly routines. Ask and answer questions.

A: I play tennis on Sunday mornings.
B: What do you do on Sunday afternoons?
A: I see my friends. We watch movies or play games. What about you?
C: On Sundays, I have lunch with my parents. In the afternoon, we talk or take a walk.

10 INTERCHANGE 6 Class survey

Find out more about your classmates.
Go to Interchange 6 on page 120.

40 Unit 6

11 READING

A Scan the interview. What's unusual about Mike's job?

What's your schedule like?

Every week, we interview someone with an unusual schedule. In this week's interview, we meet Mike Watts, a professional "sleeper." Yes, that's correct. Mike's job pays him to sleep! Here, Mike talks to us about his schedule.

News Now: Hi Mike, thanks for talking to us. What's your schedule like?
Mike: Hi there! My schedule's strange, but I love it. I go to bed at 10:00 P.M. in a different hotel room every night.
News Now: Wow! That's cool! Do you get up early?
Mike: Yes, I get up at 6:00 A.M. I'm an early bird! I like the morning. At 8:00 A.M., I have a big breakfast in the hotel restaurant.
News Now: So, who pays you to do that?
Mike: I work for a travel blog. They pay me to stay in different hotels and write about them. People read the blog and go to the hotels. Right now, I'm at a hotel in Finland, Hotel Finn.
News Now: And what do you do before you go to bed?
Mike: Every afternoon, from 2:00 P.M. to 4:00 P.M., I write about each room. I talk about the bed, the lights, the noise . . .
News Now: Who reads the blog?
Mike: Lots of different people read it. Business people, tourists, travel agencies . . . people who want to know about hotels, really!
News Now: What do you do in the evening?
Mike: At 7:00 P.M., I talk to the hotel manager. Then I go to my new room and go to bed.
News Now: Do you like sleeping?
Mike: Yes, I do! I'm very good at it!

B Read the article. Number the activities in Mike's schedule from 1 to 5. Then answer the questions. Write the times.

_____ a. Mike writes about each room.   _____ d. He goes to his new room.
__1__ b. He gets up.   _____ e. He has a big breakfast.
_____ c. He talks to the hotel manager.

1. What time does Mike write about each room? _____
2. What time does he get up? _____
3. What time does he talk to the hotel manager? _____
4. What time does he go to bed? _____
5. What time does he have breakfast? _____

C Are you an "early bird," like Mike? Or are you a "night owl"? Write five sentences about your schedule. Compare with a partner.

early bird

night owl

I ride my bike to school. **41**

Units 5–6 Progress check

SELF-ASSESSMENT

How well can you do these things? Check (✓) the boxes.

I can . . .	Very well	OK	A little
Understand times and descriptions of activities (Ex. 1)	☐	☐	☐
Ask and answer questions about present activities (Ex. 2)	☐	☐	☐
Talk about personal routines (Ex. 3)	☐	☐	☐
Ask and answer questions about routines (Ex. 4)	☐	☐	☐
Ask and answer questions about celebrities' appearances and activities (Ex. 5)	☐	☐	☐

1 LISTENING I'm calling from Los Angeles.

▶ It's 9:00 A.M. in Los Angeles. Stephanie is calling friends around the world. Listen to the conversations and complete the chart.

	1. Chelsea	2. Carlos	3. Nicholas
City	New York		
Time			
Activity			

2 SPEAKING We're on vacation!

Student A: Imagine your classmates are on vacation. Student B calls you. Ask questions about your classmates.

Student B: Imagine you are on vacation with your classmates. Call Student A. Answer Student A's questions about your classmates.

A: Hello?
B: Hi, it's . . . . I'm on vacation in . . .
A: In . . . ? Wow! What are you doing?
B: . . .
A: Who are you with?
B: . . .
A: What's he/she doing?
B: . . .
A: Well, have fun. Bye!

42

3 SPEAKING One day in my week

A Choose one day of the week and write it in the blank.
What do you do on this day? Complete the chart.

	Day:
In the morning	
In the afternoon	
In the evening	
At night	

B **PAIR WORK** Tell your partner about your routine on the day from part A.

A: On Saturdays, I exercise in the morning. I run in the park with my friends.
B: What time do you run?
A: We run at 9:00.

4 SPEAKING Lifestyle survey

A Answer the questions in the chart. Check (✓) Yes or No.

	Yes	No	Name
1. Do you live with your parents?	☐	☐	
2. Do both your parents work?	☐	☐	
3. Do you play video games at night?	☐	☐	
4. Do you eat dinner with your family?	☐	☐	
5. Do you stay at home on weekends?	☐	☐	
6. Do you work on Saturdays?	☐	☐	

B **CLASS ACTIVITY** Go around the class and find classmates with the same answers.
Write their names in the chart. Try to write a different name on each line.

5 SPEAKING Guess who!

GROUP WORK Think of a famous person. Your classmates ask
yes/no questions to guess the person.

Is it a man? a woman?   Does he/she speak English?
Does he/she live in . . . ?   Does he/she play soccer? basketball?
Is he/she a singer? an actor? Does he/she wear glasses?

WHAT'S NEXT?

Look at your Self-assessment again. Do you need to review anything?

Units 5–6 Progress check 43

7 Does it have a view?

▶ Describe houses and apartments
▶ Discuss furniture and dream homes

1 SNAPSHOT

▶ Listen and practice.

Home Sweet Home

What rooms are in houses in your country? What rooms are in apartments?
What rooms are in your house or apartment? What is your favorite room?

2 CONVERSATION Do you live downtown?

▶ Listen and practice.

Julia: Hi Ethan. Guess what! I have a new apartment.
Ethan: Hey! Cool! Do you live downtown?
Julia: No, I don't. I live near the university now.
Ethan: That's great! What's it like?
Julia: It's really nice. It has a big living room, a bedroom, a bathroom, and a kitchen.
Ethan: Awesome! Does it have an elevator?
Julia: Yes, it does.
Ethan: And does it have a nice view?
Julia: No, it doesn't. It has a view of another apartment building!

3 GRAMMAR FOCUS

> **Simple present short answers**
>
> **Do** you **live** in an apartment?　　　**Does** Ethan **live** in a house?
> Yes, I **do**. / No, I **don't**.　　　　　　Yes, he **does**. / No, he **doesn't**.
> **Do** the bedrooms **have** closets?　　　**Does** the house **have** a yard?
> Yes, they **do**. / No, they **don't**.　　　Yes, it **does**. / No, it **doesn't**.
>
> **GRAMMAR PLUS** *see page 138*

A Complete the conversation. Then practice with a partner.

Julia _____Do_____ you _____live_____ in an apartment?
Ethan No, I _____. I _____ in a house.
Julia _____ it _____ a yard?
Ethan Yes, it _____.
Julia That sounds nice. _____ you _____ alone?
Ethan No, I _____. I _____ with my family.
Julia _____ you _____ any brothers or sisters?
Ethan Yes, I _____. I _____ four sisters.
Julia Really? _____ your house _____ many bedrooms?
Ethan Yes, it _____. It _____ four.
Julia _____ you _____ your own bedroom?
Ethan Yes, I _____. I'm really lucky.

B **PAIR WORK** Read the conversation in part A again. Ask and answer these questions about Ethan.

1. Does he live in an apartment?
2. Does his house have a yard?
3. Does he live alone?
4. Does he have his own room?

C **PAIR WORK** Write five questions to ask your partner about his or her home. Then ask and answer the questions.

4 LISTENING We have a nice yard.

Listen to four people describe their homes. Number the pictures from 1 to 4.

  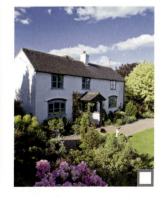 

Does it have a view? **45**

5 WORD POWER Furniture and appliances

A Listen and practice.

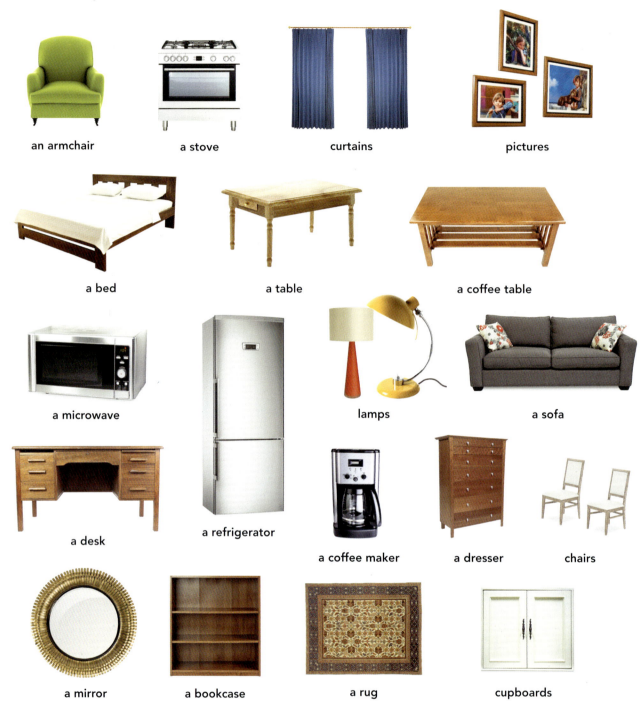

B Which rooms have the things in part A? Complete the chart.

A kitchen has . . .	a table a stove
A dining room has . . .	a table
A living room has . . .	
A bedroom has . . .	

C **GROUP WORK** What furniture is in your house or apartment? Tell your classmates.

"My living room has a sofa, a bookcase, and a rug . . ."

6 CONVERSATION I really need some furniture.

▶ Listen and practice.

Eric: This apartment is great, Lara.
Lara: Thanks. I love it, but I really need some furniture.
Eric: What do you need?
Lara: Oh, lots of things. For example, there are some chairs in the kitchen, but there isn't a table.
Eric: That's true. And there's no sofa in the living room.
Lara: And there aren't any armchairs, there isn't a rug . . . There's only this lamp!
Eric: So let's go shopping next weekend!

7 GRAMMAR FOCUS

There is, there are

There's a bed in the bedroom.
There's no sofa in the bedroom.
There isn't a table in the kitchen.

There are some chairs in the kitchen.
There are no chairs in the living room.
There aren't any chairs in the living room.

There's = There is

GRAMMAR PLUS see page 138

A Look at the picture of Ann's apartment. Complete the sentences. Then practice with a partner.

1. _There's no_ dresser in the bedroom.
2. _____ chairs in the kitchen.
3. _____ lamp in the living room.
4. _____ refrigerator.
5. _____ rugs on the floor.
6. _____ curtains on the windows.
7. _____ armchair in the bedroom.
8. _____ books in the bookcase.

B Write five sentences about things you have or don't have in your home. Then compare with a partner.

> There are two sofas in my living room.

8 INTERCHANGE 7 Find the differences

Compare two apartments. Go to Interchange 7 on page 121.

Does it have a view? **47**

9 PRONUNCIATION Words with *th*

A Listen and practice. Notice the pronunciation of /θ/ and /ð/.

/ð/ /θ/ /ð/ /ð/ /θ/ /θ/
There are **th**irteen rooms in **th**is house. **Th**e house has **th**ree ba**th**rooms.

B PAIR WORK List other words with /θ/ and /ð/. Then use them to write two sentences. Read them aloud.

There are thirty-three books on their bookcase.

10 LISTENING A furniture website

Listen to Jacob and Courtney talk about furniture on a website. What does Courtney like? What doesn't she like? Choose ☺ (likes) or ☹ (doesn't like).

☺ ☹	armchairs	☺ ☹	a sofa
☺ ☹	a rug	☺ ☹	lamps
☺ ☹	a bookcase	☺ ☹	a mirror
☺ ☹	a coffee table	☺ ☹	curtains

11 SPEAKING My dream home

A Write a description of your dream home.

What is your dream home?
Where is it?
What rooms does it have?
What things are in the rooms?
Does it have a view?

My dream home is a loft in a big city. There is one large living room with a lot of windows. There are two bedrooms and . . .

a beach house

a loft in a big city

a country villa

B PAIR WORK Ask your partner about his or her dream home.

A: What is your dream home?
B: My dream home is a loft in a big city.
A: What rooms does it have?
B: Well, there is a big living room, a small kitchen . . .

a cabin in the mountains

Unit 7

12 READING

A Scan the article. Which hotel has a room that looks like a dessert?

TRAVEL NEWS
Home   Posts   Archives

Unique Hotels

Which do you like – the world of science or the world of fiction? In this week's vacation post, we discover a hotel made for fans of nature and another hotel for fans of stories.

Bubble Hotel, Allauch, France — 4 new

Just imagine sleeping in a giant, clear bubble in a forest. That's exactly what happens here. At night, hotel guests lie in bed and watch the stars and moon. Each bubble has a comfortable bed and a nice bathroom with a shower. There's also an air-conditioner to keep the room cool in summer and a heater to keep it warm when it's cold outside.

Each bubble room is different. Guests choose the "Zen" bubble if they want to feel relaxed. Or they stay in the "Love Nature" bubble for a beautiful view. Sometimes there are rabbits and squirrels playing outside. Is there anything missing? Well, yes, there isn't a TV because no one needs a TV in a bubble!

The Roxbury, New York, the United States — 4 new

In the mountains near New York City, there's a very unusual hotel. Its name is the Roxbury. It has many rooms, but every single room is different. There's the Wizard's Emeralds room, for example. It has a yellow "road" in the middle – just like in *The Wizard of Oz*. There's a green shower in the bathroom with big red flowers on the walls.

Do you like sweet things?
Maryann's Coconut Cream Pie room looks just like a dessert – good enough to eat! The bed is round like a pie, and the ceiling looks like whipped cream.

How about space?
When you walk into George's Spacepad, you see an enormous red bathtub. It glows in the dark! There isn't a shower, but there are silver curtains, crazy lights, and two cozy sofas. It's really out of this world!

B Read the article. What's in each hotel? Complete the sentences.

| sofas | animals | moon | round bed | ✓ yellow road |
| stars | bathtub | TV | shower | air-conditioner |

At The Roxbury
1. In the Wizard's Emeralds room, there is a _____yellow road_____.
2. There is a _____ in Maryann's Coconut Cream Pie room.
3. In George's Spacepad, there are two _____. There is a red _____, but there isn't a _____.

At the Bubble Hotel
4. There is a view of the _____ and the _____.
5. There is an _____ to keep the room cool.
6. There are sometimes _____ playing outside.
7. There isn't a _____.

C **GROUP WORK** Talk about these questions.
1. Which hotel do you like? Why?
2. Imagine you have a hotel. What do you do to make it interesting?

Does it have a view? 49

8 Where do you work?

▶ Discuss jobs and workplaces using simple present Wh-questions
▶ Discuss opinions about jobs using *be* + adjective and adjective + noun

1 WORD POWER Jobs

A Match the jobs with the pictures. Then listen and practice.

a. accountant	e. doctor	i. office manager	m. security guard
b. bellhop	f. front desk clerk	✓ j. police officer	n. server
c. cashier	g. host	k. receptionist	o. taxi driver
d. chef	h. nurse	l. salesperson	p. vendor

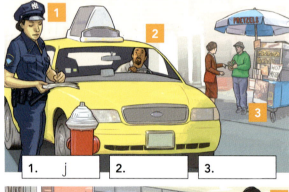

1. j   2.   3.

4.   5.   6.

7.   8.   9.

10.   11.

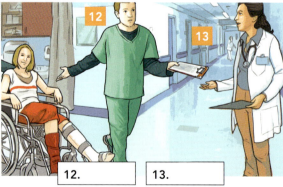

12.   13.

14.   15.   16.

B **PAIR WORK** Ask questions about the people in part A. What are their jobs?

A: What does she do?
B: She's a police officer.

50

2 SPEAKING Workplaces

A PAIR WORK Who works in these places? Complete the chart with jobs from Exercise 1. Add one more job to each list.

A: A doctor works in a hospital.   **B:** A nurse works in a hospital, too.

IN A HOSPITAL	IN AN OFFICE	IN A STORE	IN A HOTEL
a doctor			
a nurse			

B CLASS ACTIVITY Ask and answer *Who* questions about jobs. Use these words.

wears a uniform	sits all day	stands all day	works with a team
talks to people	works hard	works at night	makes a lot of money

A: Who wears a uniform?
B: A police officer wears a uniform.
C: A security guard wears a uniform, too.

3 CONVERSATION What does he do?

▶ Listen and practice.

JORDAN Where does your brother work?
ALICIA In a hotel.
JORDAN Oh, really? My brother works in a hotel, too. He's an accountant.
ALICIA How does he like it?
JORDAN He hates it. He doesn't like the manager.
ALICIA That's too bad. What hotel does he work for?
JORDAN The Plaza.
ALICIA That's funny. My brother works there, too.
JORDAN Oh, that's interesting. What does he do?
ALICIA Actually, he's the manager!

Where do you work? 51

4 GRAMMAR FOCUS

Simple present Wh-questions

Where do you **work**?	**Where does** he **work**?	**Where do** they **work**?
In a hospital.	In a hotel.	In an office.
What do you **do**?	**What does** he **do**?	**What do** they **do**?
I'm a doctor.	He's a manager.	They're accountants.
How do you **like** it?	**How does** he **like** it?	**How do** they **like** it?
I really like it.	It's OK.	They hate it.

GRAMMAR PLUS see page 139

A Complete these conversations. Then practice with a partner.

1. **A:** ____What____ does your sister ____do____ ?
   B: My sister? She's a teacher.
   A: _____ does she _____ it?
   B: It's difficult, but she loves it.

2. **A:** _____ does your brother _____ ?
   B: In an office. He's an accountant.
   A: Oh? _____ does he _____ it?
   B: He doesn't really like it.

3. **A:** _____ do your parents _____ their jobs?
   B: Oh, I guess they like them.
   A: I don't remember. _____ do they _____ ?
   B: In a big hospital. They're doctors.

4. **A:** _____ do you _____ ?
   B: I'm a student.
   A: I see. _____ do you _____ your classes?
   B: They're great. I like them a lot.

B **PAIR WORK** Ask questions about these people. Where do they work? What do they do? How do they like it?

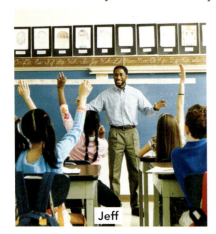
Jeff

Jodie

Chad and Tracy

A: Where does Chad work?
B: He works in . . .

5 PRONUNCIATION Reduction of *do*

Listen and practice. Notice the reduction of **do**.

Where **do you** work?   Where **do they** work?

What **do you** do?   What **do they** do?

Unit 8

6 SNAPSHOT

▶ Listen and practice.

WHAT'S YOUR JOB LIKE?

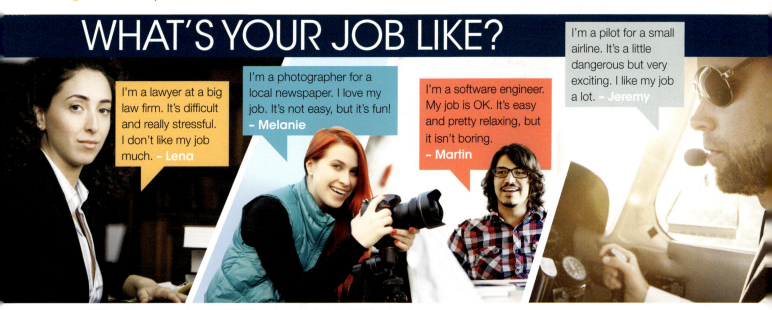

I'm a lawyer at a big law firm. It's difficult and really stressful. I don't like my job much. – **Lena**

I'm a photographer for a local newspaper. I love my job. It's not easy, but it's fun! – **Melanie**

I'm a software engineer. My job is OK. It's easy and pretty relaxing, but it isn't boring. – **Martin**

I'm a pilot for a small airline. It's a little dangerous but very exciting. I like my job a lot. – **Jeremy**

Who likes his or her job? Who doesn't? Why? Why not?
What jobs do you think are interesting? What jobs are not very interesting?

7 CONVERSATION It's a dangerous job.

▶ Listen and practice.

JACK Hey, Paula. I hear you have a new job.

PAULA Yes. I'm teaching math at Lincoln High School.

JACK How do you like it?

PAULA It's difficult, but the students are terrific. How are things with you?

JACK Not bad. Guess what! I'm a firefighter now.

PAULA Really? Wow! How do you like it?

JACK It's a dangerous job, but it's really interesting. I love it!

PAULA OK, but please be careful!

8 LISTENING Is your job interesting?

▶ Listen to four people talk about their jobs. Complete the chart with the correct jobs and adjectives.

	What do they do?	What's it like?
1. Yasmin		
2. Kana		
3. Luke		
4. Brandon		

Where do you work? **53**

9 GRAMMAR FOCUS

Placement of adjectives

be + adjective
A doctor's job **is stressful**.
A firefighter's job **is dangerous**.

adjective + noun
A doctor has **a stressful job**.
A firefighter has **a dangerous job**.

GRAMMAR PLUS *see page 139*

A Write each sentence a different way. Then compare with a partner.

1. A photographer's job is interesting. <u>A photographer has an interesting job.</u>
2. A pilot's job is exciting. _____
3. A teacher's job is stressful. _____
4. A cashier has a boring job. _____
5. An accountant has a difficult job. _____
6. A receptionist has an easy job. _____

B GROUP WORK Write one job for each adjective. Do your classmates agree?

1. easy ____actor____
2. difficult _____
3. dangerous _____
4. boring _____
5. exciting _____
6. relaxing _____

A: A graphic designer has an easy job.
B: I don't agree. A graphic designer's job is difficult.
C: I think . . .

graphic designer

10 INTERCHANGE 8 The perfect job

What do you want in a job? Go to Interchange 8 on page 122.

11 SPEAKING Workday routines

GROUP WORK Ask three classmates about their jobs (or their friends' or family members' jobs). Then tell the class.

Ask about a classmate	Ask about a classmate's friend or family member
Do you have a job?	Tell me about your . . .
Where do you work?	Where does he/she work?
What do you do, exactly?	What does he/she do, exactly?
Is your job interesting?	Is his/her job difficult?
What time do you start work?	What time does he/she start work?
When do you finish work?	When does he/she finish work?
Do you like your job?	Does he/she like his/her job?
What do you do after work?	What does he/she do after work?

Unit 8

12 READING

A Do you think all jobs are boring? Think again! Look at the photos. What do these people do?

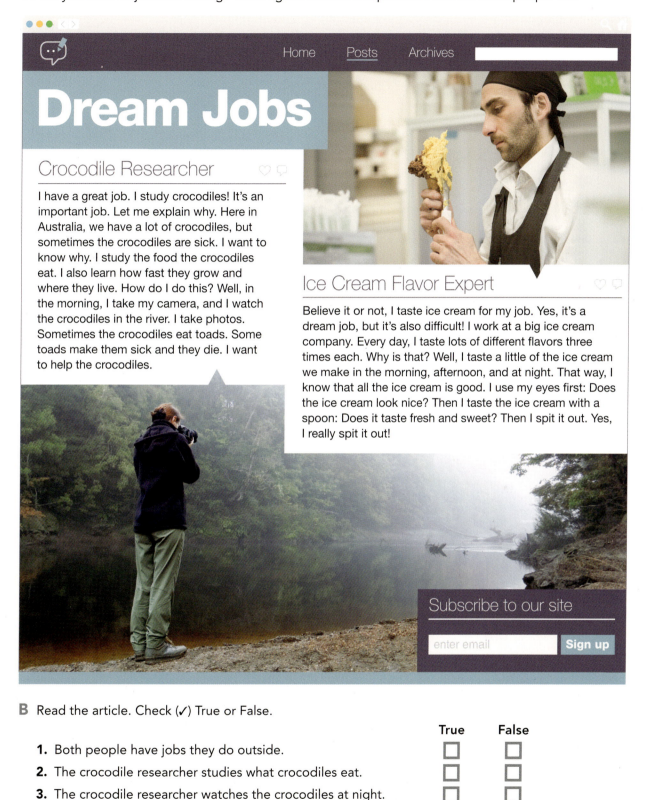

Dream Jobs

Crocodile Researcher

I have a great job. I study crocodiles! It's an important job. Let me explain why. Here in Australia, we have a lot of crocodiles, but sometimes the crocodiles are sick. I want to know why. I study the food the crocodiles eat. I also learn how fast they grow and where they live. How do I do this? Well, in the morning, I take my camera, and I watch the crocodiles in the river. I take photos. Sometimes the crocodiles eat toads. Some toads make them sick and they die. I want to help the crocodiles.

Ice Cream Flavor Expert

Believe it or not, I taste ice cream for my job. Yes, it's a dream job, but it's also difficult! I work at a big ice cream company. Every day, I taste lots of different flavors three times each. Why is that? Well, I taste a little of the ice cream we make in the morning, afternoon, and at night. That way, I know that all the ice cream is good. I use my eyes first: Does the ice cream look nice? Then I taste the ice cream with a spoon: Does it taste fresh and sweet? Then I spit it out. Yes, I really spit it out!

B Read the article. Check (✓) True or False.

	True	False
1. Both people have jobs they do outside.	☐	☐
2. The crocodile researcher studies what crocodiles eat.	☐	☐
3. The crocodile researcher watches the crocodiles at night.	☐	☐
4. The ice cream flavor expert tastes each flavor three times.	☐	☐
5. Ice cream flavor experts don't look at the ice cream.	☐	☐

C What's your dream job? Why? Write a short description. Compare with a partner.

Where do you work?

Units 7–8 Progress check

SELF-ASSESSMENT

How well can you do these things? Check (✓) the boxes.

I can . . .	Very well	OK	A little
Ask and answer questions about living spaces (Ex. 1)	☐	☐	☐
Talk about rooms and furniture (Ex. 1)	☐	☐	☐
Ask and answer questions about work (Ex. 2)	☐	☐	☐
Understand descriptions of jobs (Ex. 3)	☐	☐	☐
Give and respond to opinions about jobs (Ex. 4)	☐	☐	☐

1 SPEAKING A new apartment

A Imagine you are moving into this apartment. What things are in the rooms? Draw pictures. Use the furniture in the box and your own ideas.

> bed   chairs   desk   dresser   lamp   mirror   sofa   table

B PAIR WORK Ask questions about your partner's apartment.

A: I'm moving into a new apartment!
B: That's great! Where is it?
A: . . .
B: What's it like? Does it have many rooms?
A: Well, it has . . .

B: Does the . . . have . . . ?
A: . . .
B: Do you have a lot of furniture?
A: Well, there's . . . in the . . .
    There are some . . . in the . . .
B: Do you have everything you need for the apartment?
A: No, I don't. There's no . . .
    There isn't any . . .
    There aren't any . . .
B: OK. Let's go shopping this weekend!

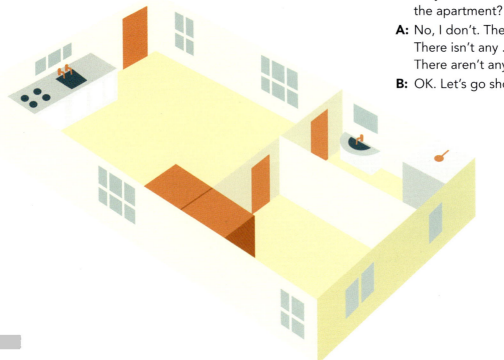

2 SPEAKING What does he do?

A Complete the conversations with Wh-questions.

1. **A:** _Where does your father work_ ?
   B: My father? He works in a store.
   A: _____ ?
   B: He's a salesperson.
   A: _____ ?
   B: He likes his job a lot!

2. **A:** _____ ?
   B: I'm an accountant.
   A: _____ ?
   B: I work in an office.
   A: _____ ?
   B: It's OK. I guess I like it.

B **PAIR WORK** Your partner asks the questions in part A. Answer with your own information.

3 LISTENING How do you like your job?

▶ Listen to Rachel, Daniel, and Mai talk about their jobs. Check (✓) the correct answers.

	Where do they work?		What do they do?	
1. Rachel	☐ office	☐ store	☐ receptionist	☐ doctor
2. Daniel	☐ hospital	☐ school	☐ nurse	☐ teacher
3. Mai	☐ hotel	☐ office	☐ manager	☐ front desk clerk

4 SPEAKING Boring or interesting?

GROUP WORK What do you think of these jobs? Give your opinions.

veterinarian

dentist

architect

hairstylist

A: I think a veterinarian has a stressful job.
B: I don't really agree. I think a veterinarian's job is relaxing.
C: Well, I think a veterinarian's job is difficult. . . .

WHAT'S NEXT?

Look at your Self-assessment again. Do you need to review anything?

Interchange activities

INTERCHANGE 1 Celebrity classmates

A Imagine you are a celebrity. Write your name, phone number, and email address on the screens.

B **CLASS ACTIVITY** Go around the class. Introduce yourself to three "celebrities." Ask and answer questions to complete the screens.

A: Hi. My name is Emma Watson.
B: I'm Usain Bolt. Nice to meet you, Emma.
A: Usain, what's your email address?
B: It's U-S-A-I-N-B-O-L-T underscore eight-seven at C-U-P dot O-R-G.
A: I'm sorry. Can you repeat that?

useful expressions

I'm sorry.
Can you repeat that?
How do you spell that?

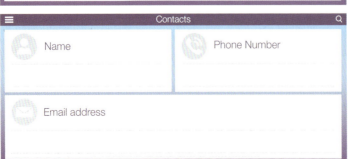

Emma Watson

Usain Bolt

114 Interchange 1

INTERCHANGE 2 Find the differences

PAIR WORK How are the two pictures different? Ask questions to find the differences.

A: Where are the sunglasses?
B: In picture 1, they're on the bicycle.
A: In picture 2, they're on the table.

Interchange 2

INTERCHANGE 4 Celebrity fashions

GROUP WORK Describe the people in the pictures. Don't say the person's name. Your classmates guess the person.

A: He's wearing blue jeans, a beige shirt, and a black jacket. Who is it?
B: Is it John Cho?

A: No, it isn't.
B: Is it Liam Hemsworth?
A: That's right.

Bradley Cooper

Rashida Jones

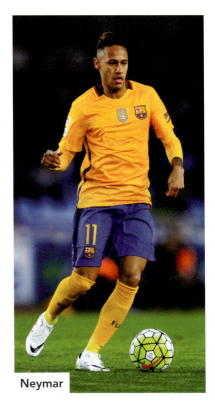
Neymar

Cristiano Ronaldo

Idris Elba

Scarlett Johansson

Ariana Grande

John Cho

Ang Lee

Kate Middleton

Zoe Saldana

Liam Hemsworth

INTERCHANGE 3 Let's talk!

A CLASS ACTIVITY Talk to your classmates. Ask two different classmates each question. Write their names and answers.

Question	Name:	Name:
What's your last name?		
Where are you from?		
What is your parents' first language?		
How do you spell your best friend's name?		
What's your best friend like?		
What is your email address?		
What is your phone number?		

B CLASS ACTIVITY Tell the class two things about your partners.

"Yumi's last name is Suzuki. Francisco is from Guatemala."

Interchange 3

INTERCHANGE 5 What's wrong with this picture?

GROUP WORK What's wrong with this picture? Tell your classmates.

"Mia and Karen are playing basketball, but they're wearing dresses!"

Interchange 5

INTERCHANGE 6 Class survey

A CLASS ACTIVITY Go around the class and find this information. Try to write a different name on each line.

Find someone who ...

	Name
gets up at 5:00 A.M. on weekdays	
gets up at noon on Saturdays	
does homework on Sunday night	
works at night	
works on weekends	
has a pet	
dances on Friday night	
lives alone	
takes a bus to class	
rides a motorcycle to class	
cooks on weekends	
plays the drums	
has two brothers	
writes emails every day	
speaks three languages	
doesn't eat breakfast	

work at night

cook on the weekends

play the drums

A: Do you get up at 5:00 A.M. on weekdays, Kun-woo?
B: No, I get up at six-thirty.
A: Do you get up at 5:00 A.M. on weekdays, Yasmin?
C: Yes, I get up at 5:00 A.M. every day.

B GROUP WORK Compare your answers.

A: Kun-woo gets up at six-thirty on weekdays.
B: Yasmin gets up at 5:00 on weekdays.
C: Lucas gets up at . . .

120 Interchange 6

INTERCHANGE 7 Find the differences

A PAIR WORK Find the differences between Tony's apartment and Nicole's apartment.

Tony's apartment

Nicole's apartment

A: There are four chairs in Tony's kitchen, but there are three chairs in Nicole's kitchen.
B: There is a sofa in Tony's living room, but there is no sofa in Nicole's living room.

B GROUP WORK Compare your answers.

Interchange 7 **121**

INTERCHANGE 8 The perfect job

A PAIR WORK Imagine you're looking for a job. What do you want to do? First, check (✓) your answers to the questions. Then ask your partner the same questions.

	Me		My partner	
Do you want to . . . ?	Yes	No	Yes	No
work from 9 to 5	☐	☐	☐	☐
work in an office	☐	☐	☐	☐
work outdoors	☐	☐	☐	☐
work at home	☐	☐	☐	☐
work with a team	☐	☐	☐	☐
use a computer	☐	☐	☐	☐
use English	☐	☐	☐	☐
travel	☐	☐	☐	☐
talk to people	☐	☐	☐	☐
help people	☐	☐	☐	☐
wear a suit	☐	☐	☐	☐
perform in front of people	☐	☐	☐	☐

work from 9 to 5

perform in front of people

work outdoors

work with a team

Positive	Negative
It's easy. / It's an easy job.	It's difficult. / It's a difficult job.
It's exciting. / It's an exciting job.	It's boring. / It's a boring job.
It's terrific. / It's a terrific job.	It's very stressful. / It's a very stressful job.
It's pretty relaxing. / It's a pretty relaxing job.	It's really dangerous. / It's a really dangerous job.

B PAIR WORK Think of a good job for your partner. Go to pages 50 and 53 for ideas.

A: You want to travel and use English. Do you want to be a pilot?

B: No, a pilot's job is very stressful.

A: OK, do you want to be . . . ?

122 Interchange 8

This page is intentionally left blank

Grammar plus

UNIT 1

1 My, your, his, her `page 3`

- Use *his* with males and *her* with females: **His** name is Travis. (NOT: ~~Her name is Travis.~~)
  Her name is Nicole. (NOT: ~~His name is Nicole.~~)

Complete the conversations with *my*, *your*, *his*, or *her*.

1. **A:** Hello. _____My_____ name is Carlos.
   B: Hi, Carlos. What's _____ last name?
   A: It's Gonzales.
   B: How do you spell _____ last name? Is it G-O-N-Z-A-L-E-Z?
   A: No, it's G-O-N-Z-A-L-E-S. And what's _____ name?
   B: _____ name is Bill Powers. Nice to meet you.

2. **A:** What's Ms. Robinson's first name?
   B: _____ first name is Elizabeth. _____ nickname is Liz.
   A: I'm sorry. What's _____ first name again?
   B: It's Elizabeth. And what's Mr. Weber's first name?
   A: _____ first name is Peter.
   B: That's right. And _____ nickname is Pete.
   A: That's right, too!

2 The verb *be* `page 5`

- In questions, the verb *be* comes before the noun or pronoun: **Are you** Joshua Brown?
  Is he in our English class? **Is she** the teacher?
- Don't use contractions in short answers with *Yes*: Are you in my class?
  Yes, **I am**. (NOT: ~~Yes, I'm.~~)

Complete the conversations with the words in the box.

am	I'm	it's	she's	you're
✓ are	I am	I'm not	you	

1. **A:** Excuse me. _____Are_____ you Layla Moore?
   B: No, _____. _____ over there.
   A: OK. Thanks.

2. **A:** Hi. Are _____ Layla Moore?
   B: Yes, _____.
   A: Nice to meet you. _____ Sergio Oliveira.
   _____ in my English class.
   B: Yes, I _____. _____ nice to meet you too, Sergio.

132 Unit 1 Grammar plus

1 This/these; it/they; plurals — page 10

- Don't use a contraction with *What + are*: **What** are these? (NOT: ~~What're these?~~)
- Use *this* with singular nouns: **This** is a laptop. Use *these* with plural nouns: **These** are flash drives.

Choose the correct words.

1. A: What's / (What are) these?
   B: It's / They're my flash drive / flash drives.
2. A: What's / What are this?
   B: It's / They're a / an cell phone.
3. A: What's this / these?
   B: It's / They're a / an English book.

2 Yes/No and *where* questions with *be* — page 11

- In questions with *where*, the verb comes after *Where*: **Where** is my credit card? (NOT: ~~Where my credit card is?~~) **Where** are my sunglasses? (NOT: ~~Where my sunglasses are?~~)

A Match the questions with the answers.

1. Is that your wallet? _c_
2. Are these your glasses? _____
3. Where are my keys? _____
4. Is this your bicycle? _____
5. Where's your tablet? _____

a. They're in your backpack.
b. No, it's not.
c. Oh, yes, it is!
d. It's on my desk.
e. No, they're not.

B Complete the conversation. Use the words in the box.

| are they | it is | they are | where |
| it | it's | this | ✓ where's |

A: ___Where's___ my dictionary?
B: I don't know. Is _____ in your backpack?
A: No, _____ not.
B: Is _____ your dictionary?
A: Yes, _____ Thanks! Now, _____ are my glasses?
B: _____ on your desk?
A: Yes, _____. Thank you!

Unit 2 Grammar plus **133**

1 Negative statements and yes/no questions with *be* page 17

- Use *be* + *not* to form negative statements: Ana **isn't** a student. (NOT: ~~Ana no is a student.~~)
- *You* is a singular and a plural pronoun: Are **you** from Rio? Yes, **I** am./Yes, **we** are.

A Unscramble the words to write negative statements.

1. is / of Canada / Toronto / the capital / not
   Toronto is not the capital of Canada.
2. Buenos Aires / not / from / we're
   _____
3. not / you and Ashley / in my class / are
   _____
4. is / my first language / Korean / not
   _____
5. from / my mother / not / is / Italy
   _____
6. my parents / not / are / they
   _____

B Complete the conversations.

1. **A:** _____Are_____ you and your friend from Costa Rica?
   B: No, _____ not. _____ from the Dominican Republic.
2. **A:** _____ your first language Spanish?
   B: Yes, it _____. My parents _____ from Ecuador.
3. **A:** _____ Nadia and Rayan Lebanese?
   B: Yes, _____ are. But _____ in France now.
4. **A:** _____ my friends and I late?
   B: No, _____ not. _____ early!

2 Wh-questions with *be* page 20

- Use *what* to ask about things. Use *where* to ask about places. Use *who* to ask about people. Use *What is/are . . . like?* to ask for a description.
- Use *how* to ask for a description: **How are** you today? Use how old to ask about age: **How old** is he?
- In answers about age, you can use only the number or the number + years old: He's **18**. OR He's **18 years old**. (NOT: ~~He has 18 years.~~)

Complete the questions with *how*, *what*, *where*, or *who*. Then match the questions with the answers.

1. _Who_ is that? _d_
2. _____ is her name? _____
3. _____ is she like? _____
4. _____ old is she? _____
5. _____ your family from? _____
6. _____ is Kyoto like? _____

a. We're from Japan – from Kyoto.
b. She's 18.
c. Her name is Hina.
d. She's my sister.
e. Oh, it's really beautiful.
f. She's very nice and friendly.

134 Unit 3 Grammar plus

1 Possessives — page 24

- The noun comes after a possessive adjective: This is **my** T-shirt.
- Don't include the noun after a possessive pronoun: This T-shirt is **mine**.
- *Whose* can be used with singular and plural nouns: **Whose** scarf is this? **Whose** sneakers are these?

Complete the conversations. Use the words in the boxes. There are two extra words in each box.

| his | mine | my | your | yours | ✓ whose |

1. **A:** ___Whose___ jacket is this? Is it _____, Ethan?
   B: No, it's not _____. Ask Matt. I think it's _____.

| her | my | mine | your | yours |

2. **A:** These aren't _____ gloves. Are they _____?
   B: No, they're not _____. Maybe they are Young-min's.

| her | hers | their | theirs | whose |

3. **A:** _____ sweaters are these? Are they Rachel's?
   B: No, they're not _____ sweaters. But these shorts are _____.

2 Present continuous statements; conjunctions — page 26

- The present continuous is the present of *be* + verb + *-ing*: It**'s raining**. She**'s wearing** a raincoat.
- The two negative contractions mean the same: **He's not/He isn't** wearing a coat. **We're not/We aren't** wearing gloves.

Change the affirmative sentences to negative sentences. Change the negative sentences to affirmative sentences.

1. Mr. and Mrs. Liu are wearing green caps. ___Mr. and Mrs. Liu aren't wearing green caps.___
2. It isn't snowing. _____
3. I'm wearing a winter coat. _____
4. You're wearing David's sunglasses. _____
5. Ayumi isn't wearing a scarf. _____

3 Present continuous yes/no questions; adjective + noun — page 27

- In questions, the present continuous is *be* + subject + verb + *–ing*: **Is** it **raining**? **Are** you **wearing** a raincoat?
- Adjectives can come before nouns or after the verb *be*: He's wearing **a blue hat**. His hat **is blue**.
- Adjectives don't have a plural form: **a green hat**; two **green hats**.

Write questions using the words in parentheses. Then complete the responses.

1. **A:** ___Is Mr. Thomas wearing a dark blue coat?___ (wear, dark blue coat)
   B: No, he _____.
2. **A:** _____ (wear, high heels)
   B: No, we _____.
3. **A:** _____ (wear, a sweater)
   B: Yes, I _____.
4. **A:** _____ (rain)
   B: Yes, it _____.

Unit 4 Grammar plus

UNIT 5

1 What time is it? / Is it A.M. or P.M.? `page 31`

■ Remember: You can say times different ways: 1:15 = *one-fifteen* OR *a quarter after one.*

Write each sentence in a different way.

1. It's a quarter to four. <u>It's three forty-five.</u>

2. It's 7:00 P.M. <u>It's seven in the evening.</u>

3. It's six-fifteen. _____

4. It's 10 o'clock at night. _____

5. It's three-oh-five. _____

6. It's twenty-five to eleven. _____

7. It's one o'clock in the morning. _____

8. It's midnight. _____

2 Present continuous Wh-questions `page 33`

■ Use the present continuous to talk about actions that are happening right now:
What **are** you **doing**? **I'm talking** to you!

■ In questions, the *be* verb comes after the question word: What **are you** doing?

■ To form the continuous of verbs ending in *–e*, drop the *e* and add *–ing*: have → having.

■ For verbs ending in vowel + consonant, double the consonant and add *–ing*: get → getting.

What are the people doing? Write conversations. Use the words in parentheses.

1. A: <u>What's Matt doing?</u> (Matt)

  B: <u>He's swimming.</u> (swim)

2. A: _____ (Jon and Megan)

  B: _____ (shop)

3. A: _____ (you)

  B: _____ (write a message)

4. A: _____ (Chris)

  B: _____ (cook dinner)

5: A: _____ (you and Tyler)

  B: _____ (watch a movie)

6: A: _____ (Sara)

  B: _____ (have pizza)

7. A: _____ (you and Joseph)

  B: _____ (study for the test)

8. A: _____ (Laura and Paulo)

  B: _____ (chat online)

136 Unit 5 Grammar plus

1 Simple present statements (page 37) and Simple present statements with irregular verbs (page 38)

- In affirmative statements, verbs with *he/she/it* end in –s: He/She **walks** to school. BUT I/You/We/They **walk** to school.
- In negative statements, use *doesn't* with *he/she/it* and *don't* with all the others: He/She/It **doesn't** live here. I/You/We/They **don't** live here.
- Don't add –s to the verb: She **doesn't live** here. (NOT: ~~She doesn't lives here.~~)

Elena is talking about her family. Complete the sentences with the correct form of the verbs in parentheses.

My family and I _____live_____ (live) in the city. We _____ (have) an apartment on First Avenue. My sister _____ (go) to school near our apartment, so she _____ (walk) to school. My father _____ (work) in the suburbs, so he _____ (drive) to his job. My mother _____ (use) public transportation – she _____ (take) the bus to her office downtown. She _____ (have) a new job, but she _____ (not like) it very much. And me? Well, I _____ (not work) far from our apartment, so I _____ (not need) a car or public transportation. I _____ (ride) my bike to work!

2 Simple present questions (page 39)

- In questions, use *does* with *he/she/it* and *do* with all the others: **Does** he/she/it get up early? **Do** I/you/we/they get up early?
- Don't add –s to the verb: Does she **live** alone? (NOT: ~~Does she lives alone?~~)

A Write questions to complete the conversations.

1. **A:** <u>Do you use public transportation?</u>
   B: Yes, I use public transportation.
2. **A:** _____
   B: No, my family doesn't eat dinner at 5:00.
3. **A:** _____
   B: No, my brother doesn't take the bus to work.
4. **A:** _____
   B: No, I don't get up late on weekends.

- Use *in* with *the morning/the afternoon/the evening*. Use *at* with *night*: I go to school **in** the afternoon and work **at** night.
- Use *at* with clock times: She gets up **at** 8:00.
- Use *on* with days: He sleeps late **on** weekends. She has class **on** Mondays.

B Complete the conversation with *at*, *in*, or *on*.

A: Does your family have breakfast together _____in_____ the morning?
B: Well, we eat together _____ weekends, but _____ weekdays we're all busy. My parents go to work early – _____ 6:30. But we eat dinner together _____ the evening, and we have a big lunch together _____ Sundays. We eat _____ noon. Then _____ the afternoon, we take a walk or go to the movies.

Unit 6 Grammar plus **137**

1 Simple present short answers — page 45

■ Remember: I/You/We/They **do/don't**. He/She/It **does/doesn't**.

Choose the correct words.

A: **Do /** (**Does**) your family **live / lives** in an apartment?
B: No, we **don't / doesn't**. We **have / has** a house.
A: That's nice. **Do / Does** your house have two floors?
B: Yes, it **do / does**. It **have / has** four rooms on the first floor. And we **have / has** three bedrooms and a bathroom on the second floor.
A: And **do / does** you and your family **have / has** a yard?
B: Yes, we **do / does**. And how about you, Tim? **Do / Does** you **live / lives** in a house, too?
A: No, I **don't / doesn't**. My wife and I **have / has** a small apartment in the city.
B: Oh. **Do / Does** you **like / likes** the city?
A: Yes, I **do / does**. But my wife **don't / doesn't**.

2 There is, there are — page 47

■ Use *there is* with singular nouns: **There's** a bed. Use *there are* with plural nouns: **There are** two chairs.
■ Use *some* in affirmative statements: There are **some** chairs in the kitchen. Use *any* in negative statements: There aren't **any** chairs in the bedroom.

Read the information about the Perez family's new house. Write sentences with the phrases in the box.

there's a	there are some
there's no	there are no
there isn't a	there aren't any

1. A living room?   Yes.
2. A dining room?   No.
3. A microwave in the kitchen?   No.
4. A table in the kitchen?   Yes.
5. Curtains on the windows? Yes.
6. Rugs on the floors?   No.
7. Closets in the bedrooms? Yes.
8. Bookcases in the bedrooms? No.

1. *There's a living room.*
2. _____
3. _____
4. _____
5. _____
6. _____
7. _____
8. _____

Unit 7 Grammar plus

1 Simple present Wh-questions — page 52

■ Use *What* to ask about things: **What do** you do? Use *Where* to ask about places: **Where do** you work? Use *How do/does . . . like . . . ?* to ask for an opinion: **How does** he **like** his job?

Complete the conversations.

1. **A:** What does your husband do ?
   B: My husband? Oh, he's a nurse.
   A: Really? Where ?
   B: He works at Mercy Hospital.
2. **A:** Where ?
   B: I work in a restaurant.
   A: Nice! What ?
   B: I'm a chef.
3. **A:** How ?
   B: My job? I don't really like it very much.
   A: That's too bad. What ?
   B: I'm a cashier. I work at a clothing store.
4. **A:** What ?
   B: My brother is a doctor, and my sister is a lawyer.
   A: How ?
   B: They work very hard, but they love their jobs.

2 Placement of adjectives — page 54

■ Adjectives come after the verb *be*: A doctor's job **is stressful**. Adjectives come before nouns: A police officer has a **dangerous job**. (NOT: A police officer has a job dangerous.)

■ Adjectives have the same form with singular or plural nouns: Firefighters and police officers have stressful jobs. (NOT: . . . have stressfuls jobs.)

Use the information to write two sentences.

1. accountant / job / boring
   An accountant's job is boring.
   An accountant has a boring job.
2. salesperson / job / stressful

3. security guard / job / dangerous

4. actor / job / exciting

5. host / job / interesting

6. nurse / job / difficult

Unit 8 Grammar plus **139**

Grammar plus answer key

Unit 1

1 *My, your, his, her*
1. A: Hello. **My** name is Carlos.
   B: Hi, Carlos. What's **your** last name?
   A: It's Gonzales.
   B: How do you spell **your** last name? Is it G-O-N-Z-A-L-E-Z?
   A: No, it's G-O-N-Z-A-L-E-S. And what's **your** name?
   B: **My** name is Bill Powers. Nice to meet you.
2. A: What's Ms. Robinson's first name?
   B: **Her** first name is Elizabeth. **Her** nickname is Liz.
   A: I'm sorry. What's **her** first name again?
   B: It's Elizabeth. And what's Mr. Weber's first name?
   A: **His** first name is Peter.
   B: That's right. And **his** nickname is Pete.
   A: That's right, too!

2 The verb *be*
1. A: Excuse me. **Are** you Layla Moore?

   B: No, **I'm not**. **She's** over there.
   A: OK. Thanks.
2. A: Hi. Are **you** Layla Moore?
   B: Yes, **I am**.
   A: Nice to meet you. **I'm** Sergio Oliveira. **You're** in my English class.
   B: Yes, I **am**. **It's** nice to meet you too, Sergio.

Unit 2

1 *This/These; it/they;* plurals
1. A: **What are** these?
   B: **They're** my flash drives.
2. A: **What's** this?
   B: **It's** a cell phone.
3. A: What's **this**?
   B: **It's an** English book.

2 Yes/No and *where* questions with *be*
A

1. c   2. e   3. a   4. b   5. d

B
A: **Where's** my dictionary?
B: I don't know. Is **it** in your backpack?
A: No, **it's** not.
B: Is **this** your dictionary?
A: Yes, **it** is. Thanks! Now, where **are** my glasses?
B: **Are** they on your desk?
A: Yes, **they are**. Thank you!

Unit 3

1 Negative statements and yes/no questions with *be*
A
2. We're not from Buenos Aires.
3. You and Ashley are not in my class.
4. My first language is not Korean. / Korean is not my first language.
5. My mother is not from Italy.
6. They are not my parents.

B
1. B: No, **are** not. **We're/We are** from the Dominican Republic.
2. A: **Is** your first language Spanish?
   B: Yes, it **is**. My parents **are** from Ecuador.
3. A: **Are** Nadia and Rayan Lebanese?
   B: Yes, **they** are. But **they're/they are** in France now.
4. A: **Are** my friends and I late?
   B: No, **you're/you are** not. **You're/You are** early!

2 Wh-questions with *be*
2. **What** is her name?   c
3. **What** is she like?   f
4. **How** old is she?   b
5. **Where** is your family from?   a
6. **What** is Kyoto like?   e

Unit 4

1 Possessives
1. A: **Whose** jacket is this? Is it **yours**, Ethan?
   B: No, it's not **mine**. Ask Matt. I think it's **his**.
2. A: These aren't **my** gloves. Are they **yours**?
   B: No, they're not **mine**. Maybe they are Young-min's.
3. A: **Whose** sweaters are these? Are they Rachel's?
   B: No, they're not **her** sweaters. But these shorts are **hers**.

2 Present continuous statements; conjunctions
2. It's snowing.
3. I'm not wearing a winter coat.
4. You're not/You aren't wearing David's sunglasses.
5. Ayumi is wearing a scarf.

3 Present continuous yes/no questions
1. B: No, **he's not/he isn't**.
2. A: **Are you wearing** high heels?
   B: No, **we're not/we aren't**.
3. A: **Are you wearing** a sweater?
   B: Yes, **I am**.
4. A: **Is it** raining?
   B: Yes, **it is**.

148   Grammar plus answer key

Unit 5

1 What time is it? / Is it A.M. or P.M.?
3. It's a quarter after six.
4. It's 10:00 P.M.
5. It's five (minutes) after three.
6. It's ten thirty-five.
7. It's one A.M.
8. It's 12:00 A.M./It's twelve (o'clock) at night.

2 Present continuous Wh-questions
2. A: What are Jon and Megan doing?
   B: They're shopping.
3. A: What are you doing?
   B: I'm writing a message.
4. A: What's Chris doing?
   B: He's cooking dinner.
5. A: What are you and Tyler doing?
   B: We're watching a movie.
6. A: What's Sara doing?
   B: She's having pizza.
7. A: What are you and Joseph doing?
   B: We're studying for a test.
8. A: What are Laura and Paulo doing?
   B: They're chatting online.

Unit 6

1 Simple present statements and Simple present statements with irregular verbs
My family and I **live** in the city. We **have** an apartment on First Avenue. My sister **goes** to school near our apartment, so she **walks** to school. My father **works** in the suburbs, so he **drives** to his job. My mother **uses** public transportation – she **takes** the bus to her office downtown. She **has** a new job, but she **doesn't like** it very much. And me? Well, I **don't work** far from our apartment, so I **don't need** a car or public transportation. I **ride** my bike to work!

2 Simple present questions
A
2. A: Does your family eat dinner at 5:00?
3. A: Does your brother take the bus to work?
4. A: Do you get up late on weekends?

B
B: Well, we eat together **on** weekends, but **on** weekdays we're all busy. My parents go to work early – **at** 6:30. But we eat dinner together **in** the evening, and we have a big lunch together **on** Sundays. We eat **at** noon. Then **in** the afternoon, we take a walk or go to the movies.

Unit 7

1 Simple present short answers
A: **Does** your family **live** in an apartment?
B: No, we **don't**. We **have** a house.
A: That's nice. **Does** your house have two floors?
B: Yes, it **does**. It **has** four rooms on the first floor. And we **have** three bedrooms and a bathroom on the second floor.
A: And **do** you and your family **have** a yard?
B: Yes, we **do**. And how about you, Tim? **Do** you **live** in a house, too?
A: No, I **don't**. My wife and I **have** a small apartment in the city.
B: Oh. **Do** you **like** the city?
A: Yes, I **do**. But my wife **doesn't**.

2 *There is, there are*
2. There's no / There isn't a dining room.
3. There's no / There isn't a microwave in the kitchen.
4. There's a table in the kitchen.
5. There are some curtains on the windows.
6. There are no / There aren't any rugs on the floors.
7. There are closets in the bedrooms.
8. There are no / There aren't any bookcases in the bedroom.

Unit 8

1 Simple present Wh-questions
1. A: Really? Where **does he work**?
2. A: Where **do you work**?
   B: I work in a restaurant.
   A: Nice! What **do you do**?
   B: I'm a chef.
3. A: How **do you like your job**?
   B: My job? I don't really like it very much.
   A: That's too bad. What **do you do**?
   B: I'm a cashier. I work at a clothing store.
4. A: What **do your brother and sister do**?
   B: My brother is a doctor, and my sister is a lawyer.
   A: How **do they like their jobs**?
   B: They work very hard, but they love their jobs.

2 Placement of adjectives
2. A salesperson's job is stressful.
   A salesperson has a stressful job.
3. A security guard's job is dangerous.
   A security guard has a dangerous job.
4. An actor's job is exciting.
   An actor has an exciting job.
5. A host's job is interesting.
   A host has an interesting job.
6. A nurse's job is difficult.
   A nurse has a difficult job.

Grammar plus answer key **149**

Credits

The authors and publishers acknowledge the following sources of copyright material and are grateful for the permissions granted. While every effort has been made, it has not always been possible to identify the sources of all the material used, or to trace all copyright holders. If any omissions are brought to our notice, we will be happy to include the appropriate acknowledgements on reprinting and in the next update to the digital edition, as applicable.

Texts

The Roxbury for the adapted text on p. 49. Reproduced with kind permission; Attrap'Rêves for the adapted text on p. 49. Reproduced with kind permission.

Key: B = Below, BL = Below Left, BC = Below Centre, BR = Below Right, B/G = Background, C = Centre, CL = Centre Left, CR = Centre Right, Ex = Exercise, TC = Top Centre, T = Top, TL = Top Left, TR = Top Right.

Illustrations

337 Jon (KJA Artists): 24, 29, 85; **Mark Duffin**: 15, 12(T), 31(T), 44(T), 47, 115, 121; **Thomas Girard** (Good Illustration): 3, 11, 13, 23, 25, 36, 37, 50, 79(T), 89, 100, 102; **Dusan Lakicevic** (Beehive Illustration): 21, 41, 87; **Quino Marin** (The Organisation): 26, 31(B), 79(B); **Gavin Reece** (New Division): 27, 44(B), 45, 101; **Gary Venn** (Lemonade Illustration): 56, 88, 90, 91, 127, 128; **Paul Williams** (Sylvie Poggio Artists): 9, 30, 119.

Photos

Back cover (woman with whiteboard): Jenny Acheson/Stockbyte/GettyImages; Back cover (whiteboard): Nemida/GettyImages; Back cover (man using phone): Betsie Van Der Meer/Taxi/GettyImages; Back cover (woman smiling): PeopleImages.com/DigitalVision/GettyImages; Back cover (name tag): Tetra Images/GettyImages; Back cover (handshake): David Lees/Taxi/GettyImages; p. v: PhotoAlto/Sigrid Olsson/PhotoAlto Agency RF Collections/GettyImages; p. 2 (header), p. vi (unit 1): Paul Bradbury/OJO Images; p. 2 (CR): Paul Bradbury/Caiaimage/GettyImages; p. 2 (BL): Stefania D'Alessandro/WireImage/GettyImages; p. 2 (BR): Steve Granitz/WireImage/GettyImages; p. 4 (Ex 7.1): Maskot/Maskot/GettyImages; p. 4 (Ex 7.2): Design Pics/Ron Nickel/GettyImages; p. 4 (Ex 7.3): Dan Dalton/Caiaimage/GettyImages; p. 4 (Ex 7.4): Squaredpixels/E+/GettyImages; p. 5 (T): Fabrice LEROUGE/ONOKY/GettyImages; p. 5 (C): Erik Dreyer/The Image Bank/GettyImages; p. 5 (B): theboone/E+/GettyImages; p. 6: Maskot/Maskot/GettyImages; p. 7 (T): Peter Dazeley/Photographer's Choice/GettyImages; p. 7 (Ex 14.1): Tim Robberts/The Image Bank/GettyImages; p. 7 (Ex 14.2): Klaus Vedfelt/DigitalVision/GettyImages; p. 7 (Ex 14.3): Nicolas McComber/E+/GettyImages; p. 7 (Ex 14.4): Ariel Skelley/Blend Images/GettyImages; p. 8 (header), p. vi (unit 2): John Slater/Stockbyte/GettyImages; p. 8 (backpack): igor terekhov/iStock/GettyImagesPlus; p. 8 (cellphone): Peter Dazeley/Photographer's Choice/GettyImages; p. 8 (hairbrush): slobo/E+/GettyImages; p. 8 (sunglasses): Fodor90/iStock/GettyImages; p. 8 (wallet): bibikoff/E+/GettyImages; p. 8 (keys): Floortje/E+/GettyImages; p. 8 (umbrella): Picheat Suviyanond/iStock/GettyImages; p. 8 (energy bar): Juanmonino/iStock/Getty Images Plus/GettyImages; p. 8 (book): Image Source/Image Source/GettyImages; p. 8 (notebook): kyoshino/E+/GettyImages; p. 8 (pen): Ann Flanigan/EyeEm/Fuse/GettyImages; p. 8 (eraser): subjug/iStock/GettyImages; p. 8 (clock): GoodGnom/DigitalVision Vectors/GettyImages; p. 9 (tablet): daboost/iStock/Getty Images Plus/GettyImages; p. 9 (box): Guy Crittenden/Photographer's Choice/GettyImages; p. 9 (phone case): Jeffrey Coolidge/DigitalVision/GettyImages; p. 9 (television): Cobalt88/iStock/GettyImages; p. 9 (newspaper): -Oxford-/E+/GettyImages; p. 9 (Id): Daniel Ernst/iStock/Getty Images Plus/GettyImages; p. 9 (clip): Steven von Niederhausern/E+/GettyImages; p. 9 (ticket): Gediminas Zalgevicius/Hemera/GettyImages; p. 9 (purse): Stramyk/iStock/GettyImages; p. 10 (flash drive): zentilia/iStock/Getty Images Plus/GettyImages; p. 10 (laptop): Coprid/iStock/Getty Images Plus/GettyImages; p. 10 (laptops.): karandaev/iStock/GettyImages; p. 10 (keys): krungchingpixs/iStock/GettyImages; p. 10 (backpacks): pavila/iStock/GettyImages; p. 10 (umbrella): Kais Tolmats/E+/GettyImages; p. 10 (sunglasses): Zaharia_Bogdan/iStock/GettyImages; p. 10 (wallet): malerapaso/iStock/GettyImages; p. 10 (window): beright/iStock/GettyImages; p. 10 (credit card): freestylephoto/iStock/GettyImages; p. 10 (headphones): tiler84/iStock/GettyImages; p. 12 (backpack): JulNichols/E+/GettyImages; p. 12 (flash drive): Garsya/iStock/GettyImages; p. 12 (laptop): Creative Crop/Photodisc/GettyImages; p. 12 (newspaper): goir/iStock/GettyImages; p. 12 (computer): AlexLMX/iStock/GettyImages; p. 12 (chair): urfinguss/iStock/GettyImages; p. 12 (wallet): pioneer111/iStock/GettyImages; p. 12 (notebook): drpnncpp/iStock/GettyImages; p. 12 (tv): selensergen/iStock/GettyImages; p. 12 (glasses): bonetta/iStock/GettyImages; p. 15 (cellphone): Manuel Faba Ortega/iStock/GettyImages; p. 15 (cellphones): sunnycircle/iStock/GettyImages; p. 15 (purse): penguenstok/E+/GettyImages; p. 15 (purses): iulianvalentin/iStock/GettyImages; p. 15 (wallet): Nyo09/iStock/GettyImages; p. 15 (wallets): alarich/iStock/GettyImages; p. 16 (header), p. vi (unit 3): stock_colors/iStock/Getty Images Plus/GettyImages; p. 16 (T): Photography by ZhangXun/Moment/GettyImages; p. 16 (BL): Roberto Westbrook/Blend Images/GettyImages; p. 17 (T): Robert Frerck/The Image Bank/GettyImages; p. 17 (B): Jane Sweeney/The Image Bank/GettyImages; p. 18 (Ex 5.1): Dan MacMedan/WireImage/GettyImages; p. 18 (Ex 5.2): Steve Granitz/WireImage/GettyImages; p. 18 (Ex 5.3): Clasos/CON/LatinContent Editorial/GettyImages; p. 18 (Ex 5.4): Koki Nagahama/Getty Images AsiaPac/GettyImages; p. 18 (Ex 5.5): Jeff Spicer/Getty Images Entertainment/GettyImages; p. 19 (TR): SolStock/E+/GettyImages; p. 19 (cellphone): Peter Dazeley/Photographer's Choice/GettyImages; p. 19 (Ben): Hero Images/Hero Images/GettyImage; p. 19 (Nadia): Portra Images/DigitalVision/GettyImages; p. 19 (Ex 7.c.a): Fuse/Corbis/GettyImages; p. 19 (Ex 7.c.b): Purestock/GettyImages; p. 19 (Ex 7.c.c): Lucy Lambriex/Moment/GettyImages; p. 19 (Ex 7.c.d): James Woodson/Photodisc/GettyImages; p. 19 (Ex 7.c.e): Fuse/Corbis/GettyImages; p. 20 (Ex 8.a.1): Alex Barlow/Moment/GettyImages; p. 20 (Ex 8.a.2): Jupiterimages/Stockbyte/GettyImages; p. 20 (Ex 8.a.3): PhotoAlto/Frederic Cirou/PhotoAlto Agency RF Collections/GettyImages; p. 20 (Ex 8.a.4): Hill Street Studios/Blend Images/GettyImages; p. 22 (header), p. vi (unit 4): Sam Edwards/Caiaimage/GettyImages; p. 22 (formal man): Spiderstock/E+/GettyImages; p. 22 (formal woman): Grady Reese/E+/GettyImages; p. 22 (rain coat): EdnaM/iStock/Getty Images Plus/GettyImages; p. 22 (coat): DonNichols/E+/GettyImages; p. 22 (dress): ARSELA/E+/GettyImages; p. 22 (casual woman): BLOOM image/BLOOMimage/GettyImages; p. 22 (pajamas): madtwinsis/E+/GettyImages; p. 22 (swimwear): dendong/iStock/Getty Images Plus/GettyImages; p. 22 (shorts): 487387674/iStock/Getty Images Plus/GettyImages; p. 22 (cap): Steve Zmina/DigitalVision Vectors/GettyImages; p. 25 (brazilian flag): Image Source/Image Source/GettyImages; p. 25 (japanese flag): Jim Ballard/Photographer's Choice/GettyImages; p. 25 (american flag): NirdalArt/iStock/GettyImages; p. 25 (canadian flag): Encyclopaedia Britannica/UIG/Universal Images Group/GettyImages; p. 25 (TL): Andrea Pistolesi/Photolibrary/GettyImages; p. 25 (TR): Photograph by Kangheewan/Moment Open/GettyImages; p. 25 (BL): Bruce Leighty/Photolibrary/GettyImages; p. 25 (BR): EschCollection/Photonica/GettyImages; p. 25 (thermometer): Burke/Triolo Productions/Stockbyte/GettyImages; p. 29: PeopleImages.com/DigitalVision/GettyImages; p. 30 (header), p. vi (unit 5): Driendl Group/Photographer's Choice/GettyImages; p. 30 (Brian): Daniel Grill/GettyImages; p. 30 (Amar): Peter Cade/The Image Bank/GettyImages; p. 31 (Ex 3.a.1): Raimund Koch/The Image Bank/GettyImages; p. 31 (Ex 3.a.2): Science Photo Library/Science Photo Library/GettyImages; p. 31 (Ex 3.a.3): Paul Bricknell/Dorling Kindersley/GettyImages; p. 31 (Ex 3.a.4): SergeiKorolko/iStock/GettyImages; p. 31 (Ex 3.a.5): pagadesign/iStock/GettyImages; p. 31 (Ex 3.a.6): scanrail/iStock/GettyImages; p. 32 (T): Plume Creative/DigitalVision/GettyImages; p. 32 (BR): B. Sporrer/J.Skowronek/StockFood Creative/GettyImages; p. 32 (Jay): B. Sporrer/J.Skowronek/StockFood Creative/GettyImages; p. 32 (Kate): Rafael Elias/Moment Open/GettyImages; p. 33 (TL): Tetra Images/Brand X Pictures/GettyImages; p. 33 (TC): Hola Images/GettyImages; p. 33 (TR): Tim Robberts/The Image Bank; p. 33 (CL): annebaek/iStock/Getty Images Plus/GettyImages; p. 33 (C): Stockbyte/Stockbyte/GettyImages; p. 33 (CR): Caiaimage/Tom Merton/Caiaimage/GettyImages; p. 33 (BL): LWA/Sharie Kennedy/Blend Images/GettyImages; p. 33 (BC): sot/DigitalVision/GettyImages; p. 33 (BR): David Crunelle/EyeEm/EyeEm/GettyImages; p. 34 (dance): Blend Images - Ariel Skelley/GettyImages; p. 34 (drive): Westend61/Westend61/GettyImages; p. 34 (music): Hero Images/Hero Images/GettyImages; p. 34 (basketball): Daniel Grill/Tetra images/GettyImages; p. 34 (read): Peathegee Inc/Blend Images/GettyImages; p. 34 (bycycle): Daniel Milchev/The Image Bank/GettyImages; p. 34 (run): Ty Milford/Aurora Open/GettyImages; p. 34 (shop): BJI/Blue Jean Images/blue jean images/GettyImages; p. 34 (study): JAG IMAGES/DigitalVision/GettyImages; p. 34 (swim): J J D/Cultura/GettyImages; p. 34 (walk): Dougal Waters/Photographer's Choice RF/GettyImages; p. 34 (movie): Blend Images/Andres Rodriguez/Blend Images/GettyImages; p. 35 (Eva35): Sebastian Doerken/fStop/GettyImages; p. 35 (PamL): Denis Schneider/EyeEm/EyeEm/GettyImages; p. 35 (TL): Hero Images/Hero Images/GettyImages; p. 35 (BR): Betsie Van Der Meer/Taxi/GettyImages; p. 36 (header), p. vi (unit 6): Enrique Díaz/7cero/Moment/GettyImages; p. 36 (Ex 1.1): Image Source/DigitalVision/GettyImages; p. 36 (Ex 1.2): Kentaroo Tryman/Maskot/GettyImages; p. 36 (Ex 1.3): Susanne Kronholm/Johner Images Royalty-Free/GettyImages; p. 36 (Ex 1.4): Eternity in an Instant/The Image Bank/GettyImages; p. 36 (Ex 1.5): Marilyn Nieves/iStock/GettyImages; p. 36 (Ex 1.6): Matt Dutile/Image Source/GettyImages; p. 36 (Ex 1.7): Ciaran Griffin/Stockbyte/GettyImages; p. 36 (Ex 1.8): Maria Teijeiro/DigitalVision/GettyImages; p. 38: Robert Daly/Caiaimage/GettyImages; p. 39: Michael Berman/DigitalVision/GettyImages; p. 40: Frank van Delft/Cultura/GettyImages; p. 41: vadimguzhva/iStock/GettyImages; p. 42 (man): James Whitaker/DigitalVision/GettyImages; p. 42 (woman): Tyler Stableford/The Image Bank/GettyImage; p. 43: Pingebat/DigitalVision Vectors; p. 44 (header), p. vi (unit 7): Peter Adams/Photolibrary; p. 45 (lobby): piovesempre/iStock/GettyImages; p. 45 (apartment): Joe_Potato/iStock/GettyImages; p. 45 (house): Ron Evans/Photolibrary/GettyImages; p. 45 (kitchen): ttatty/iStock/GettyImages; p. 46 (armchair): xiaoke ma/E+/GettyImages; p. 46 (stove): taist/iStock/GettyImages; p. 46 (curtains): darksite/iStock/GettyImages; p. 46 (pictures): Glow Decor/Glow/GettyImages; p. 46 (bed): Emevil/iStock/GettyImages; p. 46 (coffee maker): GeorgePeters/E+/GettyImages; p. 46 (table): EdnaM/iStock/GettyImages; p. 46 (coffee table): DonNichols/E+/GettyImages; p. 46 (oven): mbbirdy/E+/GettyImages; p. 46 (refrigerator): JazzIRT/E+/GettyImages; p. 46 (lamps1): Creative Crop/DigitalVision/GettyImages; p. 46 (lamps2): stuartbur/E+/GettyImages; p. 46 (sofa): AnnaDavy/iStock/GettyImages; p. 46 (desk): Hemera Technologies/PhotoObjects.net/GettyImages; p. 46 (bookcase): DonNichols/iStock/GettyImages; p. 46 (dresser): Hemera Technologies/PhotoObjects.net/GettyImages; p. 46 (chairs): Firmafotografen/iStock/Getty Images Plus/GettyImages; p. 46 (mirror): Omer Yurdakul Gundogdu/E+/GettyImages; p. 46 (rug): DEA/G. CIGOLINI/De Agostini Picture Library/GettyImages; p. 46 (cupboards): ChoochartSansong/iStock/GettyImages; p. 47: Marco Baass/GettyImages; p. 48 (loft): Martin Barraud/OJO Images/GettyImages; p. 48 (mountains): Barrett & MacKay/All Canada Photos/GettyImages; p. 48 (villa): Maremagnum/Photolibrary/GettyImages; p. 48 (beach house): catnap72/E+/GettyImages; p. 49 (T): BERTHIER Emmanuel/hemis.fr/hemis.fr/GettyImages; p. 49 (B): Michael Marquand/Lonely Planet Images/GettyImages; p. 50 (header), p. vi (unit 8): iStock/Getty Images Plus/GettyImages; p. 51 (hospital): Vincent Hazat/PhotoAlto Agency RF Collections/GettyImages; p. 51 (office): Peopleimages/E+/GettyImages; p. 51 (store): Maskot/Maskot/GettyImages; p. 51 (hotel): DAJ/amana images/GettyImages; p. 51 (BR): Nevena1987/iStock/GettyImages; p. 51 (Jorden): Sam Edwards/OJO Images/GettyImages; p. 51 (Alicia): Philipp Nemenz/Cultura/GettyImages; p. 52 (BL): Digital Vision./DigitalVision/GettyImages; p. 52 (BC): PeopleImages/DigitalVision/GettyImages; p. 52 (BR): Glow Images, Inc/Glow/GettyImages; p. 53 (lawyer): rubberball/GettyImages; p. 53 (pilot): Katja Kircher/Maskot/GettyImages; p. 53 (photographer): stock_colors/E+/GettyImages; p. 53 (engineer): Thomas Barwick/Iconica/GettyImages; p. 53 (BR): Rubberball/Mike Kemp/Brand X Pictures/GettyImages; p. 53 (Paula): Marc Romanelli/Blend Images/GettyImages; p. 54 (T): Hero Images/Hero Images/GettyImages; p. 54 (B): Jetta Productions/Stone/GettyImages; p. 55 (B): Australian Scenics/Photolibrary/GettyImages; p. 55 (T): Eugenio Marongiu/Cultura/GettyImages; p. 57 (veterinarian): fotoedu/iStock/GettyImages; p. 57 (dentist): XiXinXing/XiXinXing/GettyImages; p. 57 (architect): John Lund/Marc Romanelli/Blend Images/GettyImages; p. 57 (hairstylst): Glow Images, Inc/Glow/GettyImages; p. 114 (CR): Pascal Le Segretain/Getty Images Entertainment/GettyImages; p. 114 (BR): Amanda Edwards/WireImage/GettyImages; p. 116 (Bradley Cooper): Steve Granitz/WireImage/GettyImages; p. 116 (Rashida Jones): Stefanie Keenan/WireImage/GettyImages; p. 116 (Neymar): David Ramos/Getty Images; p. 116 (Ronaldo): Anthony Harvey/Getty Images Entertainment/GettyImages; p. 116 (Idris Elba): Dave J Hogan/Getty Images Entertainment/GettyImages; p. 116 (Scarlett Johansson): Ray Tamarra/WireImage/GettyImages; p. 117 (Ariana Grande): Christopher Polk/Getty Images Entertainment/GettyImages; p. 117 (John Cho): John M. Heller/Getty Images Entertainment/GettyImages; p. 117 (Ang Lee): Pascal Le Segretain/Getty Images Entertainment/GettyImages; p. 117 (Kate Middleton): Anwar Hussein/WireImage/GettyImages; p. 117 (Zoe Saldana): Jon Kopaloff/FilmMagic/GettyImages; p. 117 (Liam Hemsworth): Joe Scarnici/Getty Images Entertainment/GettyImages; p. 118: PeopleImages.com/DigitalVision/GettyImages; p. 120 (TR): Garry Wade/The Image Bank/GettyImages; p. 120 (CR): Indeed/ABSODELS/GettyImages; p. 120 (BR): Joos Mind/Photographer's Choice/GettyImages; p. 122 (CR): urbancow/iStock/GettyImages; p. 122 (TR): George Doyle/Stockbyte/GettyImages; p. 122 (BL): Dennis K. Johnson/Lonely Planet Images/GettyImages; p. 122 (BR): baona/E+/GettyImages